"The single best investment you can make in your professional image."

Chris Hammer, MBA, Stanford University,
Management Consultant

"You step with competitive confidence when you Master Your Professional Image."

Patricia Plant, Legal Arbitrator, Facilitator, Mediator

"An invaluable resource for professionals."

Sondra Carmody, Hotel Employee/Labor Relations Manager

"A blueprint for dressing with visual integrity."

Rita George, Marketing Strategist and Founder of The Edge

"I find these sensible techniques to be an invaluable part of being effective in business today."

Janet Ralston, Vice President, Marketing,
Advanced Medical Nutrition, Inc.

"The concepts in this book have helped me minimize purchases while maximizing the diversity of my wardrobe."

Jill Armstrong Hope, Ph.D., Professor at San Francisco State University,
Former President of the San Francisco Opera Guild

"Provides everything you need to know to develop and fine-tune your professional image."

Robin Stavinsky, Managing Partner,
New Venture Marketing

Mastering Your Professional Image™

Dressing to Enhance Your Credibility

Diane Parente & Stephanie Petersen

Illustrations by Jan Mucklestone

Edited by Karen Johnson and Sherry K. Brennan, M.Ed.

Design and Electronic Production by Terry Marc Hardy of E-ARTS

Image Development and Management, Inc.

Mastering Your Professional Image™
DRESSING TO ENHANCE YOUR CREDIBILITY

Diane Parente and Stephanie Petersen

Illustrations by Jan Mucklestone

Edited by Karen Johnson and Sherry K. Brennan, M.Ed.

Design and Electronic Production by Terry Marc Hardy of E-ARTS of San Anselmo, California

Published by Image Development and Management, Inc.

Post Office Box 262, Ross, California 94957

415 258-0285

FAX 415 485-1793

ISBN: 0-9646688-0-7

Library of Congress Catalog Number: 95-77376

Printed in the United States

Dedication

To our clients, colleagues, and friends who have provided a wealth of information and assistance in developing the concepts and material for this book. And to our husbands, who have given us continuous love and support. Without each of these contributions, *Mastering Your Professional Image* would never have been possible.

Contents

Introduction

Today is the day of that important meeting you have labored on so hard, fine-tuning your presentation down to the last detail. It is 6 a.m. when you open your closet and panic. You think: What am I going to wear? I need to create a good impression. Should I stay with something conservative? Maybe distinctive is better, but understated may be good, too! I want people to listen and to ask questions, so I need to be approachable as well. What am I going to do?

With all the options available, dressing can be a confusing and challenging venture. Wearing clothes that convey the appropriate message reinforces your credibility, enhances your self-confidence, and makes a more positive impression on others. Visual perception is an essential element in good communication. Your image is what sets you apart and is one of your best marketing tools.

In the 1990s women are changing the way they look and how they present themselves in business. John Molloy's book, *Dress for Success*, is no longer the key to the boardroom. Dressing in a skirted-suit with a bow-tie blouse for all business situations is too limiting and unflattering. You need not look like a man to succeed in business — just look at Carol Bartz, Chief Executive Officer of Autodesk; Connie Chung, journalist and national television news anchor; and Mae Jemison, medical doctor and the first African-American woman in space. All of these women dress with visual integrity in clothing that reinforces what they do and who they are. The way you dress directly influences how others perceive you. This is a reality that you cannot afford to ignore.

The need for a positive and consistent public image leads many companies to struggle with the idea of casual days, those days when employees are not held to strict business dress codes. Many companies are concerned that such informality will undermine their well-established image without producing an appreciable increase in employee morale. When IBM announced it was trading in its blue-suit-and-white-shirt uniform and allowing employees to wear casual clothes five days a week, the announcement sent shock waves through the national business community. Articles began to appear in newspapers and magazines debating the crisis in business dressing and corporate image. Although it is possible to wear more relaxed fashions and still maintain an air of dignity and good taste, too many people are confusing casual with sloppy, and undermining the image their companies have so carefully constructed. What you wear to work is not a mindless daily routine but one that needs careful consideration. A well-defined, deliberate business wardrobe will provide you with the tools necessary to enhance your visual presentation, making you a more effective communicator. It is hard to succeed in any business or profession without communicating a clear and confident message.

An effective image need not cost a queen's ransom or take a lifetime to complete. A meaningful wardrobe strategy can save you money by eliminating unnecessary purchases or poor choices. Further, it can give you the gift of time so desperately needed in today's fast-paced world. For most women shopping is no longer entertainment. The shop-till-you-drop phenomenon is part of the bygone 1980s. Also, tighter finances have made maintaining an overstuffed closet of seldom-worn clothes unrealistic.

Mastering Your Professional Image can help maximize your visual presentation in a variety of business situations by:

- Identifying your image options and how each style of dressing can benefit you and maintain your company's integrity, even on dress-down days

- Enhancing your look through careful use of fit, shape, color, fabric, accessories, and grooming

- Addressing special situations and events

- Developing a plan for investing in a winning wardrobe

- Managing your investment for years of timeless and effective dressing

So, on to *Mastering Your Professional Image!*

Defining Your Options

Defining Your Options

How you dress makes an impression on others - one that can be a major asset or stumbling block. You are no longer limited to a single professional look, but the new range of choices can be just as frustrating. Now you have the opportunity to select a visual image that advances your ideas and effectiveness. To create a positive professional image, you need to properly address all details, from head to toe, giving others a clear impression of your seriousness, skill, and sense of responsibility. Selecting the appropriate look will add to your professional demeanor by allowing others to focus on what you are saying rather than what you are wearing.

To dress appropriately, you must consider several variables, namely the industry, who you will be interacting with, how you want to be perceived, the location, and time. For instance, you may need a particular look for a financial business meeting on Wall Street, another for delivering a sales presentation to a retail industry group, and a completely different look for organizing or attending a computer fair in Las Vegas.

Enhancing your visual presentation and credibility begins with *Mastering Your Professional Image* by:

- Selecting an appropriate style (the proper mix of color, fabric, and shape) for the desired visual message

- Achieving a good fit

- Coordinating all garments and accessories (shoes, hosiery, handbags, scarves, jewelry, eye frames, and hair ornaments)

- Understanding what it means to be well-groomed

To unlock the door to maximizing your professional image, you need to understand the differences between the seven basic style options. There are four Classic style options: Traditional, Elegant, Dramatic, and Sporty. These are the most widely accepted for conventional business. The remaining three style options, known as the Non-Classic styles, are Feminine, Alluring, and Creative. The Non-Classic styles are more appropriate for less conventional or non-business situations. Each style has its own merit, and one is not inherently superior to another; however, greater emphasis is placed on the four Classics.

Each of the seven basic styles has its own special characteristics. Subtle differences in the use of color, shape, cut of the garment, and texture create the unique message for each style. Understanding these differences will allow you to take the guesswork out of dressing for business.

To select the appropriate Classic style, you need to ask yourself the following questions:

Question	Dressing Option
Do I want to be perceived as a conscientious, conservative team player who fits in with the group?	Traditional
Do I need to look refined and stately in order to take subtle but firm control of the situation or event?	Elegant
Do I need to be distinctive, stand out in the crowd, or attract attention?	Dramatic
Do I have some freedom to be and look more relaxed, approachable, and comfortable?	Sporty

It is likely that you have a position or career that offers you opportunities to use one or more of these dressing options. For that very reason *Mastering Your Professional Image* offers you guidelines to create the right look for a variety of situations. Also, you may find that combining elements of two styles will bring out more of your personality. These combinations are relatively simple to achieve by altering the use of color, fabric, or accessories.

The case studies preceding each style type are based upon composites of actual women and are designed to help you understand how the manner of dressing changes for different situations.

Classic Styles

Classic styles represent the look most often worn in the business community. The four Classics include: Traditonal, Elegant, Dramatic, and Sporty. Slight differences in color, fabric, or shape of clothing takes you from one style to another.

TRADITIONAL:
conservative

Do I want to be perceived as a conscientious, conservative team player who fits in with the group?

Case Study 1:

Carol has been an accountant at a major financial firm for most of her career. She likes her work and aspires to gain more responsibility and authority and to move up within the ranks of her department. Often Carol works with others in the firm and enjoys the teamwork and congenial atmosphere.

Case Study 2:

Judy left her position as a middle manager at a food products firm to raise her two children. Now, after being home for many years, she is returning to work and wants to pick up where she left off. She enjoys the business world but is most interested in balancing work and home, so she wants a look that does not require a great deal of thought but is appropriate for the office environment.

Traditional is the most appropriate style for both Carol and Judy.

Defining the Traditional Style:

Traditional dressing creates the perception of a conscientious team player through its conservative and tailored styling and its emphasis on functionality rather than on the ornamental qualities of clothes and accessories. Within this style you will find clothes that can be worn for several years without becoming dated because of their versatile and timeless qualities. It is a moderate style, neither too casual nor too dressy.

The Traditional Clothing Shape:

Traditional style, born of a combination of male business fashion and timeless styling, de-emphasizes the feminine form by concealing many of the natural lines and curves of a woman. The result is a modified rectangular form. The shape has:

- Formed shoulders

- Slightly defined waist

- Ease of fit

- Modest hemlines

Clothing Design:

The building blocks of a Traditional wardrobe include:

- Jackets, suits (often single, double-breasted, collarless or blazer styles) and coats constructed with built-in support (shoulder pads, lining, and interfacing similar to menswear)

- Coordinating tailored blouses in standard styles (notched, jewel, pointed, stand-up collar, or ascot at the neck) or sweaters (turtleneck, jewel neck or V-neck with a scarf) that complement the jacket

- Skirts in either a slim fit, with some tucks at the waist (referred to as a dirndl) or a slightly fuller design; both without excessive detail

- Tailored pleated trousers

- Dresses either in one or two pieces

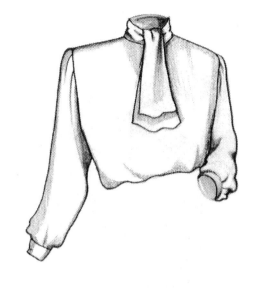

Best Fabric Choices:

Traditional fabrics are smooth to slightly textured, firm, and of medium weight and matte finish. Suit fabrics are naturals and blends that include woolens, tweeds, cavalry twills, gabardine, flannel, serge, raw silk, and heavy cottons. Blouse fabrics are blends, silk, and heavy cotton. Dresses are typically made of the same fabrics as blouses, as well as of challis, gabardine, and linen blends.

Patterns:

Prints, in small to medium scale, are generally paisleys, checks, plaids, and stripes. Most garments are in solid colors with patterns introduced for interest (for example, on a blouse, skirt, or jacket).

Colors:

Coats, suits, and jackets are purchased in neutral colors: navy, gray, all shades of beige and brown, forest green, and burgundy. Blouses and dresses are complementary, in shades of white, cream, red, navy, or pale yellow. Again, prints are acceptable if they are understated and have a theme color that matches the jacket.

Coordinating the Style:

Keeping in mind that Traditional dressing is conservative and functional, you can achieve the look with:

- A semi-fitted jacket, the cornerstone of the look, purchased separately for use with coordinates or as part of a matched suit. Stay with a medium-weight fabric

- Blouses in a conservative contrasting color with long sleeves and a notched collar. Stay with fabrics such as cotton, heavy silk, or rayon

- Tailored pants to match the jacket, or a dress that follows the same ideas noted above for a blouse; this will give you a fully coordinated look

Traditional Clothing Labels:

Here are a few well-known labels that tend to include garments that represent Traditional style:

- Anne Klein
- Anne Klein II
- Ann Taylor
- Barry Bricken
- Burberrys
- Dana Buchman
- Doncaster
- Evan Picone
- J.H. Collectibles
- J.G. Hook
- Jones of New York
- Pendleton
- Talbots

Coordinating the Accessories:

• Accessories are subtle and inconspicuous, such as:

- a minimum of two items of jewelry (excluding watch or wedding ring) in a combination of either earrings and necklace (20" to 24") or earrings and pin. Your best choices are gold and pearls

- belts made of smooth leather that match or coordinate with the skirt or pants

- shoes of medium height (no greater than a two-inch heel) in a pump or loafer style. Flats are also appropriate. Choose a solid color, multi-color, or spectator, and a style that coordinates well with the skirt or pants

- handbags that are medium sized and structured in shape, in either a shoulder or satchel style. Ideally, you will have at least two different colored bags, one for spring and summer and the other for fall and winter (for example taupe for spring and summer, and navy for fall and winter)

- scarves bearing prints similar to those found on men's ties

- watch with a round face and leather band

- hosiery in skin-toned color

- eye frames with a modified square shape

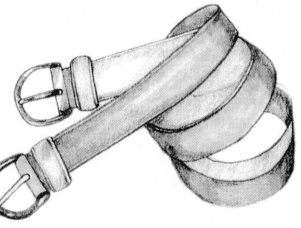

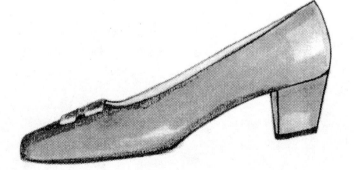

Combination Styles

Although you may prefer Traditional dressing, you can personalize or vary the look by incorporating elements of another Classic style. Here are a few ideas for altering the basic Traditional look, take a navy two-piece skirted-suit, cream-colored blouse, moderate-heel pumps, 20 to 24 inch strand of pearls, and gold and/or pearl earrings:

Elegant:
- jewel neck blouse in the same color as the jacket
- matching accessories, preferably earrings and a choker style necklace
- handbag and hosiery in the same color as your shoes

Dramatic:
- bold stripe blouse
- large earrings, no necklace
- belt with an obvious buckle

Sporty:
- pleated pants
- neckline of the blouse worn open
- flat shoes

ELEGANT: refined

Do I need to look refined and stately in order to take
subtle but firm control of the situation or event?

Case Study 1:
Ellen, once a researcher supporting high-powered negotiators, has been promoted and is now a contract negotiator. This new role requires Ellen to project an image of a highly confident, experienced professional who represents a prestigious organization. Ellen does not want to be perceived as assertive but rather as a cool, calm authority figure whose comments are to be taken very seriously.

Case Study 2:
Patricia recently graduated with a master's degree in government studies and is hoping to make a career in politics, focusing on foreign affairs. She works at the local district office of the United States Department of State and is occasionally invited to attend luncheons and meetings with foreign dignitaries. Although she is not in line for appointment as an ambassador to a foreign country, she is preparing herself to be considered for such a post. So, in addition to sharpening her skills in foreign languages, politics, and customs, she wants to create the dignified external image that is suited to her position.

The Elegant look is the most appropriate for both Ellen and Patricia.

Defining the Elegant Style:

To create a visual image of stately refinement with subtle but firm control of each situation, Elegant dressing emphasizes formality. All the elements of the look are meticulously tailored of subtly colored, luxurious fabrics. It is a style based on ensemble dressing, where all of the pieces match or blend harmoniously. A great deal of thought goes into the selection of each garment and accessory.

The Elegant Clothing Shape:

The most feminine of the classic styles, Elegant echoes and reinforces the softly structured shape of the feminine form. The result is a perfect, graceful fit characterized by:

• Slightly shaped shoulders

• Gentle definition of the waist

• Well-fitted styling

• Discreet, not extreme hemlines

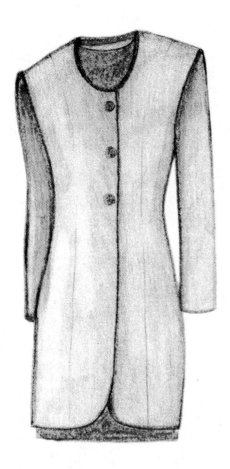

Clothing Design:

Style basics include:

- Suits and coats with light, hidden support, high-quality interfacing and lining, slim shapes and soft tailoring. Collars are more rounded than angular. Jacket styles include tunic, double- and single-breasted, and collarless.

- Blouses or sweaters with uncluttered necklines and set-in sleeves

- Matching slim, smooth, straight skirts; or highly tailored pants with uncomplicated waistlines. All skirts and most pants are fully lined

- Dresses are unadorned, slightly defined at the waist and may have a matching jacket, or in a coat style

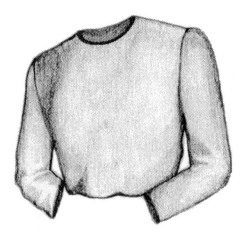
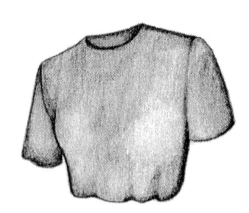

Best Fabric Choices:

Most Elegant clothing is fashioned from luxurious, superior-quality natural fabrics or high-quality blends in medium to light weight, with a smooth surface. The beauty and grace of the fabric is the focus of the garment. This tendency for high quality leads to higher prices, a factor that must be given a great deal of consideration when putting together an Elegant wardrobe. You will be making a long-term commitment and investment in each ensemble.

Fabrics are of light to medium weight. There is a subtle sheen or patina to the fabric; it is never dull or overly shiny. Suit fabrics include gabardine, wool crepe, closely woven knits, silk shantung, camel hair, and fine silks as well as wools from Italy and England. Blouses are made of silk crepe de chine, pima cotton, fine wool, and challis. Dresses are often of the same fabric as blouses, and may include cashmere and wool jersey. Pants are gabardine, wool crepe, silk, and linen blend.

Patterns:

Elegant style is most often seen in solid colors; it occasionally incorporates a pattern within the color in low to medium contrast, such as a tone-on-tone jacquard or subdued marbling. Subtle designs, crests, fleur-de-lys, or status logos may appear on accessories.

Colors:

Essential wardrobe items such as coats and suits are purchased in subtle, light or dark neutrals, with a monochromatic theme. Some of the more prevalent colors are cream, beige, taupe, mauve, pearl gray, sea mist green, slate blue, ink navy, and black. The monochromatic theme is sometimes interrupted by varying the shades. Avoid strong contrasts, keeping colors within a couple of shades of the focus color.

Coordinating the Style:

Keeping in mind that the look is one of refinement and formality, you should select:

- All of the elements of an ensemble at the same time to ensure effective matching

- An understated suit in wool gabardine or crepe

- Softly tailored blouses in the same general color as the other major garments, in solid colors or tone-on-tone jacquard pattern with a jewel or surplus neckline

Elegant Clothing Labels:

Here are some well-known labels that tend to include garments that represent the Elegant style:

- Armani
- Bill Burns
- Calvin Klein
- Christian Dior
- Ferragamo
- Jaeger
- Paul Stanley
- St. John
- Valentino

Coordinating the Accessories:

• Accessories such as:

- – matched earrings and necklace, or
  earings and a pin, in rounded shapes and satin finish

- – shoes of medium height (no greater than a two-inch
  heel) in a pump or sling, or designer flats. Both the shoes
  and the handbag should match the color and formality of
  the ensemble

- – sheer tint hosiery in a color closely matching the suit

- – a belt of smooth fine leather with a leather- or fabric-
  covered buckle, also in the same color as the ensemble

- – scarves of fine silk with designer motifs

- – eye frames and watches with a graceful oval or round shape

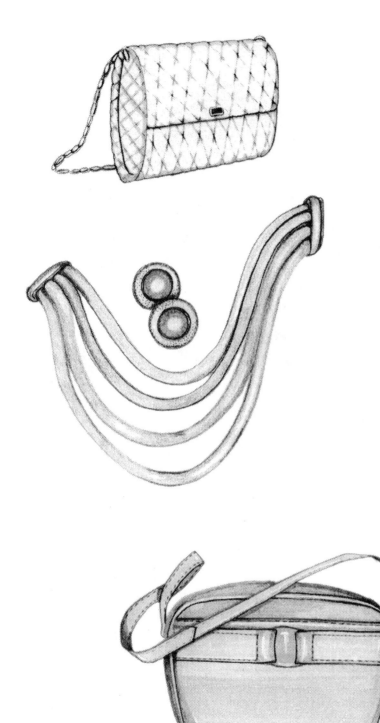

Combination Styles

Although you may prefer Elegant dressing, you can personalize or vary the look by incorporating elements of another Classic style. Here are a few ideas for altering the basic Elegant look, take a pale gray matched suit with slim skirt, pearl necklace and earring set, and coordinated shoes and handbag:

Traditional:
- pleated skirt
- mildly contrasting colored blouse
- handbag and shoes in a complementary rather than matching color

Dramatic:
- big pin on the jacket
- larger earrings, no necklace
- contrasting colored scarf draped around the neck

Sporty:
- pleated or plain front pants instead of the skirt
- flatter shoes
- cotton blouse instead of silk blouse

DRAMATIC: distinctive

Do I need to be distinctive, stand out in the crowd or
attract attention?

Case Study 1:
Donna was recently promoted to the presidency of a national industry board and needs to present herself in a commanding and powerful manner. Her work is often conducted before an audience or in large groups, so she wants a visual image that sets her apart from others. Boldness and assertiveness are more important for her than elegance or understatement.

Case Study 2:
Erica recently ventured out to develop her own company and finds that she spends a great deal of time marketing her ideas though networking activities and public speaking. In dealing with others, she wants to be distinctive and remembered.

The answer for both Donna and Erica is to add Dramatic styling to their wardrobes.

Defining the Dramatic Style:

Dramatic styling through its use of striking and sophisticated clothing and accessories, allows you to exude power and influence while standing apart from others. This style incorporates highly structured shapes of firm fabrics, generally stressing bold contrast of color. The emphasis is on exaggerated shapes. As with Elegant dressing, a great deal of thought goes into the look, so finding just the right wardrobe elements can be time-consuming and expensive. However, once you have the pieces, it is easy to assemble the outfit.

The Dramatic Clothing Shape:

Dramatic styling begins with a semi-fitted form, moving to an inverted triangle; shoulders are wide and the hem is tapered. The style is characterized by:

- Shaped and extended shoulders
- Slight or no waist definition
- Narrow fit through the hips
- Tapered hemlines

Clothing Design:

Style basics include:

- Jackets and coats that are well-constructed and have built-in support; shoulder pads extend beyond the natural ends of the shoulders and have a square shape; lapels are notched or peaked and often oversized. Jacket and suit styles include tunic, single- or double-breasted, collarless, asymetrical, or cropped.

- Tops are typically the focus of bold contrast and may include strong patterns, or an extreme "V," or a high-neck. Blouses or shirts have firm collars that can be worn up or down.

- Sweaters are usually high-necked (that is, turtle-neck) or V-shaped

- Dresses have elongated shapes with sharp edges; many have an asymmetrical design or strong contrasts of two or more colors

- Pants and skirts are extreme, either straight and narrow, or full

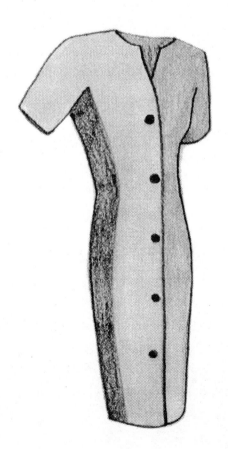

Best Fabrics Choices:

Dramatic clothes are of firm and closely woven fabrics with substantial body that helps them hold their shape. Often garments are made from natural fibers and blends with a smooth stiff finish. You may also choose matte, shiny, or glittery finishes. Suit and dress fabrics include wool gabardine, linen, heavy knits, leather, and velvet. Blouses are often made of silk, cotton broadcloth, or rayon.

Patterns:

Popular patterns include stylized prints; abstracts; geometrics; oversized, widely spaced designs; and bold stripes. Just be careful the outfit does not become too "busy" and lose its impact.

Colors:

This very important element adds emphasis to each garment or accessory. Essential wardrobe items are always in a striking color such as black, white, or a bold jewel tone (namely, purple, fuschia, red, teal, yellow, royal blue, and emerald green). Although black and white are the basic contrasting colors, any light versus dark contrast may be worn. The contrast comes from the clothes, the accessories, or both.

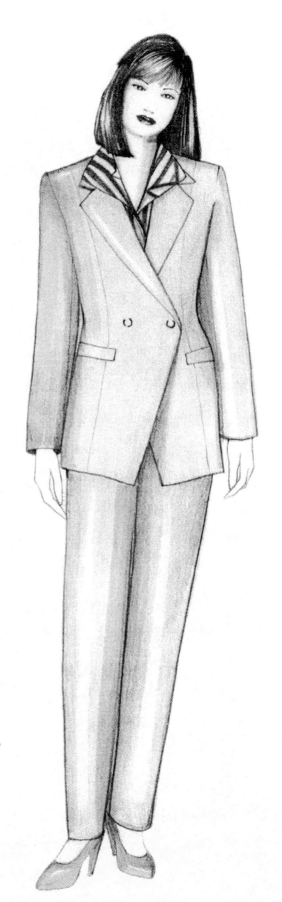

Coordinating the Style:

Keeping in mind that Dramatic dressing is striking and sophisticated, you can achieve the look with:

- A sleek gabardine suit with square broad shoulders

- Blouses in a contrasting color or with a bold pattern, such as an awning stripe. Try for exaggeration of the collar and perhaps interesting placement of the buttons or other closures

It would be wise to find a good dressmaker to custom tailor pieces that cannot be found at your favorite stores.

Dramatic Clothing Labels:

Here are some well-known labels that tend to include garments that represent Dramatic style:

- A.S.L. Kasper
- Bicci, New York
- Chetta B
- Donna Karan
- Ellen Tracy
- Escada
- Ferre
- PSI by Alvin Bell
- Tahari
- Versace
- Yves Saint Laurent

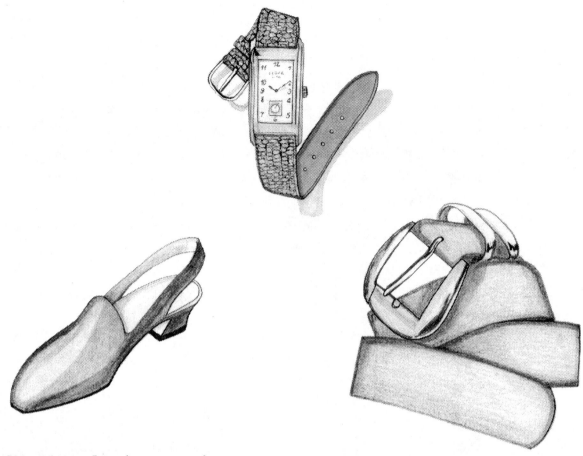

Coordinating the Accessories:

• Accessories are bold and large, with one striking piece as the dominant accessory:

  – oversized earrings, watches, and scarves

  – a statement pin

  – stylized pumps or slings (high vamp, square, or very pointed toe) perhaps with contrast or accent heels; heels are either high or flat

  – either a large or small firm-sided, structured handbag or tote in a color to match the suit or jacket

  – a belt with a noticeable buckle

  – hosiery that blends with the outfit or contrasts with the outfit, either dark or light

  – highly stylized eye frames, perhaps in a bold color or pattern

Combination Styles

Although you may prefer Dramatic dressing, you can personalize or vary the look by incorporating elements of another Classic style. Here are a few ideas for altering the basic Dramatic look, take a black suit with white blouse, stylized pumps, large earrings, and important pin:

Traditional:
- paisley silk scarf worn around the neck
- moderate earrings
- medium-heel pumps

Elegant:
- wear the suit as a two-piece dress
- matching earrings and necklace instead of a pin
- matching handbag and shoes

Sporty:
- leave jacket unbuttoned
- sweater or knit shell in place of blouse
- smaller earrings, no pin

SPORTY: relaxed

Do I have some freedom to be and look more
relaxed, approachable, and comfortable?

Case Study 1:
Sally is an energetic, talented computer software developer who often spends hours working on the details of her newest project. She likes to dress comfortably and in an unpretentious manner. She feels that her standard attire is too relaxed for the occasional meetings that she needs to attend with clients, so she is looking for a style that is comfortable without looking sloppy.

Case Study 2:
Sarah is an architect who is getting more assignments that require both client contact and on-site inspections on the same day. Although she feels that architects can be relaxed with their clothing choices, she wants a look that is polished enough for the client meeting, but also constructed for comfort and ease of movement, especially for the visits to construction sites.

The Sporty style is best for both Sally and Sarah.

Defining the Sporty Style:

Sporty styling projects an approachable, relaxed image with comfort and practicality being the main focus. This style features unrestricted tailoring in natural fabrics, typically in neutral, bright and rich colors. It is a look based on unmatched separates that are coordinated into many appropriate outfits. Sporty's unstudied, practical nature makes it particularly easy to shop for individual items. This style works best for women who work in unstructured environments.

The Sporty Clothing Shape:
Sporty style tends to disguise rather than accentuate the feminine form. It is based on:

• Natural shoulders

• Slight or no emphasis of the waist

• Comfortable fit

• Hemline defined by need for movement

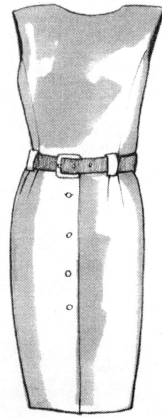

Clothing Design:

The basics of the Sporty style include the following characteristics:

- Jackets are roomy with minimum built-in support and are often worn with the sleeves rolled or pushed up. Popular styles include blazers, cardigans, single- or double-breasted, and bomber jackets

- Shirts and sweaters are loose, roomy, and can be used for layering. Necklines are nonrestrictive and often left open

- Pants, the mainstay of the wardrobe, can come in a variety of lengths and styles

- Skirts, when worn, can be either above the knee or longer, and straight or pleated

- Dresses are nonbinding, often with many detail features (button, pockets, epaulets, and/or pleats)

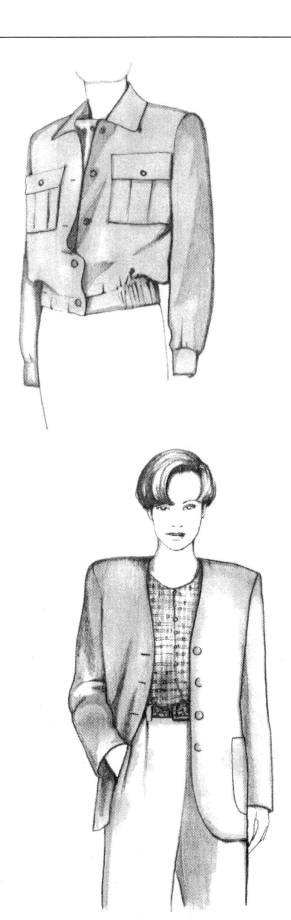

Best Fabric Choices:

The fabric's are sturdy, easy care, medium to heavier weight, and often slightly textured with surface interest. Matte finishes are preferred over shiny ones. Fabrics for jackets, skirts, or pants are natural (or the look of natural), such as camel hair, flannel, suede, challis, raw silk, linen, tweed, and basically any cotton. Blouses and dresses are in cotton, linen, and challis.

Patterns:

So popular are patterns, that an outfit can sometimes contain a combination of two or more. Dominant types include small scale, evenly spaced representational patterns, plaids, checks, polka dots, stripes, nature motifs, madras, and tartans. Patterns are most often found on shirts and sweaters.

Color:

Unlike the other styles mentioned, the Sporty look encompasses a vast array of color choices. Main garments are in neutral, rich, or bright colors, such as navy, tan, olive, khaki, red, or white. Shirts, sweaters, scarves, and other accents can be bright (red, blue, green, yellow, and orange), pastel (softer shades of the brights), or rich (olives, gold, sage, and brown), although white is also possible. Other colors can be introduced through mixing various garments or adding accessories. It is not unusual for a Sporty look to combine three or more colors in one outfit. This is your opportunity to show vitality and enthusiasm through your choice of color.

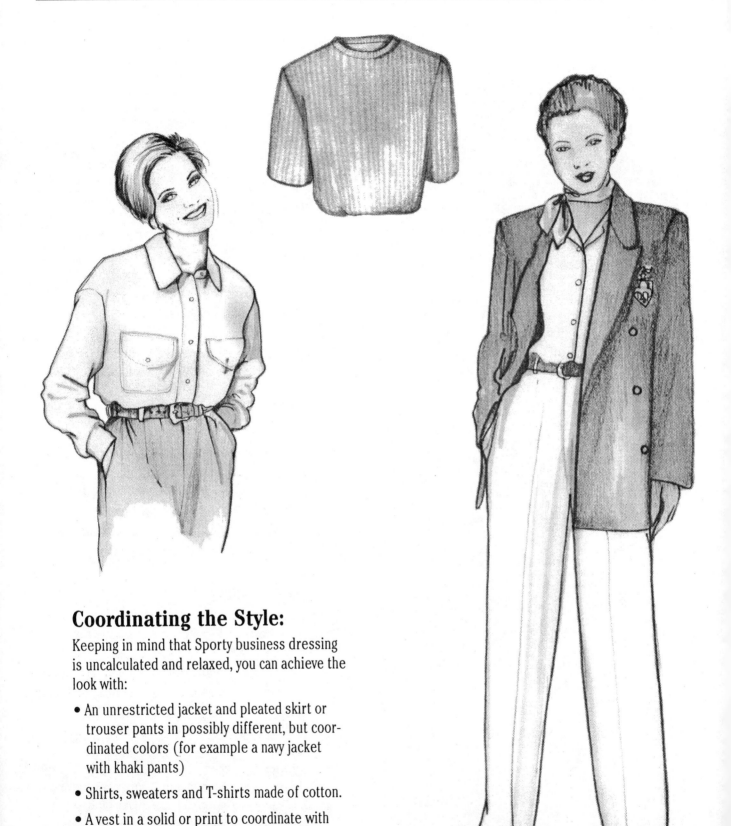

Coordinating the Style:

Keeping in mind that Sporty business dressing is uncalculated and relaxed, you can achieve the look with:

- An unrestricted jacket and pleated skirt or trouser pants in possibly different, but coordinated colors (for example a navy jacket with khaki pants)

- Shirts, sweaters and T-shirts made of cotton.

- A vest in a solid or print to coordinate with the jacket, skirt, or pants

Sporty Clothing Labels:

Here are some well-known labels that tend to include garments that represent Sporty style:

- Adrienne Vittadini
- Banana Republic
- Calvin Klein Sport
- Company/Ellen Tracy
- DKNY
- GAP
- J. Crew
- Liz Claiborne
- Lizsport
- Ralph Lauren

Coordinating the Accessories:

• Accessories are small scale, simple, lightweight, and limited in number if worn at all:

- earrings are of button or loop style that can be worn with everything

- watches have larger faces with colored fabric or springy metal band

- low heel pumps or flats with slight texture

- durable and compact shoulder handbag or backpack

- scarves are cotton or heavy silk in a square shape. Also, you can use small scarves as pocket squares for your jacket

- belts are adjustable and narrow, in a textured, woven, or top-stitched style

- hosiery in natural tones. Knee highs are preferred under pants

- eye frames are designed in a variety of styles and colors

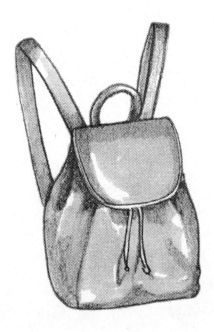

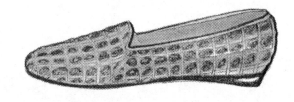

Combination Styles

Although you may prefer Sporty dressing, you can personalize or vary the look by incorporating elements of another Classic style. Here are few ideas for altering the basic Sporty look, take a navy blazer, white cotton shirt, tan pants, flat shoes, and small earrings:

Traditional:
- tan-colored straight skirt, mid-knee length or longer
- gold chain necklace
- mid-heel pumps in color matching the jacket

Elegant:
- straight skirt in color and fabric to match the jacket
- silk shell in a color closely matching the jacket
- pumps that match the outfit

Dramatic:
- pulled up shirt collar and large pin at the neck
- add a bold geometric pattern oblong scarf
- large button earrings

Non-Classic Styles

Although the Non-Classic styles - Feminine, Alluring, and Creative, are often inappropriate for conventional business environments, you can nonetheless incorporate some of these style elements into the Classics by adjusting color, fabric, fit, or accessories. Also, Non-Classic styles are great for after hours.

FEMININE: genteel

Defining the Feminine Style:

A Feminine style adds dimensions of gentility and softness and creates a feeling of warmth and compassion. This less structured style features light-weight fluid fabrics and pastel colors. It is a look that evokes a feeling of sensitivity and supportiveness. A feminine wardrobe consists of suits or dresses, either single garments or two pieces worn together. The gentleness of this style may not be assertive enough for many businesswomen, since it does not project the forcefulness needed to handle many conventional business situations. However, it may be appropriate for certain businesses or professions, such as direct home sales, therapy, or teaching elementary school. However, its more traditional role is in social settings that focus on home, church, school, club, weddings, and dating. The soft, flowing fabrics, pastel colors and small prints are romantic and cast the woman in a soft glow. In addition, the disarming quality of feminine clothing helps establish bonds with others, especially when doing volunteer work with children and the elderly.

The Feminine Clothing Shape:

Feminine styling, emphasizes a loose hour-glass that modestly conceals the feminine form.

- Soft shoulders
- Gentle definition to the torso
- Modest, below-the-knee hemline.

Coordinating the Style:

Keeping in mind that feminine dressing has curved lines with delicate details, you can achieve the look by selecting:

- A suit with a short jacket (cropped or peplum styles with slightly defined waist)

- A short wool crepe jacket with a rounded lapel worn over a patterned dress or full skirt

- Soft blouses or sweaters with detailed necklines

- Dresses may have a defined, raised, or drop-waist

- Accessories such as:

  - sheer pastel-colored hosiery

  - delicate earrings and necklace

  - antique pin

  - belts in supple leathers and fabrics

  - an unstructured clutch handbag that picks up the color of the dress or jacket

  - scarves with small, delicate patterns

  - bowed pumps with delicate heel or flat shoes

  - eye frames with thin rims

Two of the better-known labels that tend to include garments with a Feminine design are Laura Ashley and Albert Nipon.

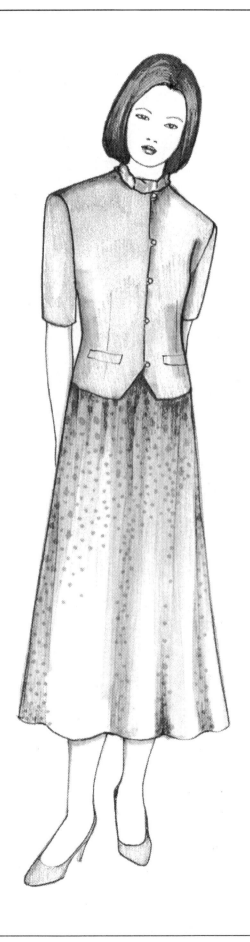

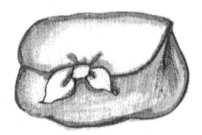

Combination Styles:

If your preferred style is Feminine, you may need to incorporate more Classic styling to provide you with an appropriate business look. Here are some suggestions on how to enhance your wardrobe for business:

- Select jackets and suits of firmer fabrics in stronger business colors, such as slate blue, gray, or taupe

- Avoid dresses with empire waistlines, puff shoulders, and frilly, or lacey collars

- Wear skin-toned hosiery

- Select medium-heel, plain pumps or closed-toe slings. It may be wise to avoid bows or other shoe ornaments

If, despite these changes, your wardrobe is still not appropriate for your career or business, you may benefit by changing gears and following the guidelines in Classic dressing, paying special attention to Elegant style.

ALLURING: glamorous

Defining the Alluring Style:

Women who want to add some daring to their image are apt to choose alluring clothes. This style incorporates body-contouring fashions made from clinging fabrics. It is a look that, because of its attention to the female form, evokes a feeling of sensuousness and excitement. An alluring wardrobe is based on dresses and close-fitting skirts and pants; each piece covers the body like a second skin. The suggestive nature of the style makes it largely inappropriate for most businesswomen because it undermines their credibility. If you choose to dress in an alluring style for business, it is very important that you control and balance the look with one of the Classic styles to counteract any negative effects.

Alluring clothes are often seen in the entertainment industry, nightclubs, bars, restaurants, and any place people gather for the evening. It is important to assess your figure honestly before selecting this look; tight garments on a full figure or untoned body can be unattractive.

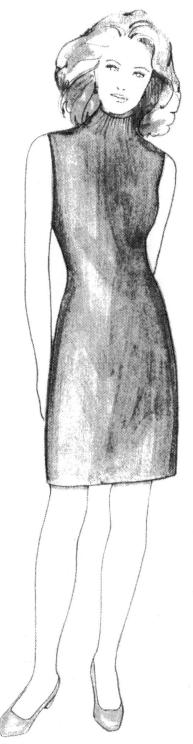

The Alluring Clothing Shape:

Alluring creates a glamorous presence by focusing attention on body curves and shapely legs. Highly fitted clothing is the norm, with hemlines on the shorter side of the current fashion.

- Natural shoulders
- Waist emphasis
- Tapered hemline

Coordinating the Style:

An Alluring look is created by selecting:

• A jacket with strong emphasis on the waist

• A blouse, sweater, or dress with a deep "V" or scoop neckline in knit or jersey

• Slim pants or skirt in a bold color such as red or black

• Accessories such as:

  – small, rounded clutch in suede, calfskin, or other supple fabric

  – minimum jewelry of moderate size

  – a wide belt, in soft stretchy material

  – black or skin-toned sheer hosiery worn with sling-back, low-cut, high-heel shoes

Two of the better known labels for Alluring style are Victoria's Secret and Andrea Jovine designs.

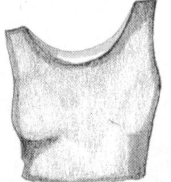

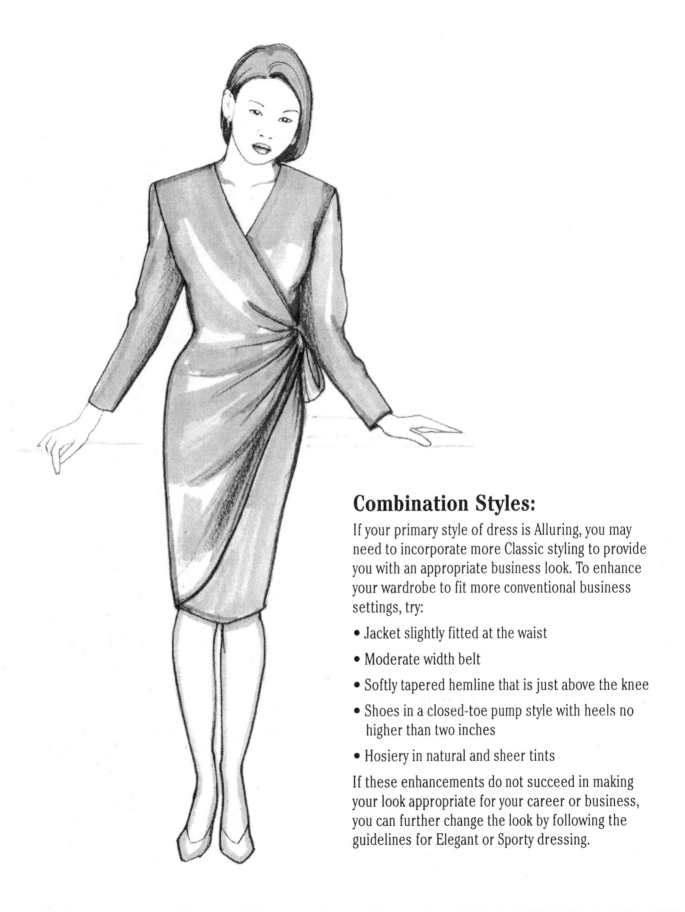

Combination Styles:

If your primary style of dress is Alluring, you may need to incorporate more Classic styling to provide you with an appropriate business look. To enhance your wardrobe to fit more conventional business settings, try:

• Jacket slightly fitted at the waist

• Moderate width belt

• Softly tapered hemline that is just above the knee

• Shoes in a closed-toe pump style with heels no higher than two inches

• Hosiery in natural and sheer tints

If these enhancements do not succeed in making your look appropriate for your career or business, you can further change the look by following the guidelines for Elegant or Sporty dressing.

CREATIVE: imaginative

Where individuality or artistic flair is important, Creative styling allows you to develop a look that is exclusively yours. It is a mixture of anything and everything; it combines any style type, Classic or Non-Classic, in an artistic manner. Creative clothing evokes a feeling of spontaneity and independence. It is often achieved by combining mismatched garments in a way that somehow works. A Creative wardrobe contains a combination of many unusual colors, textures, patterns, or designs. This style may be inappropriate for many businesses and careers, although some elements may be retained in even the most conservative environments.

Defining the Creative Style:

There are no rules to developing a Creative look; basically, if you feel it looks good, wear it. The only caveat is that you understand your environment and adjust your uniqueness to fit the situation. Although army boots and chiffon skirts may be appropriate for a modern art gallery salesperson, they may be too outrageous for an advertising or architectural firm. Many women who wear Creative clothing are involved in fashion, cosmetology, and entertainment.

In summarizing the look, it is safe to say that the clothing takes its cue from how the pieces are put together, not from individual pieces. One trademark of Creative dressing is the use of dark colors, especially black. Occasionally, there may be a murky jewel tone or splash of color. The focus will almost always be on unusual combinations.

Some favorite patterns are batik, ethnic, and dark florals. It is not unusual to see a Creative woman mix and match several unrelated patterns in one outfit (such as plaid with stripes, florals with geometrics, or polka dots with paisley).

Coordinating the Style:

Follow your instincts, but make sure the result will be acceptable in your work environment. If your outfit speaks louder than words, it may drown out what you have to say. This can be deadly in many, if not all, business dealings.

To achieve a Creative image or enhance the Classics, you can incorporate one of the following ideas:

- Adding full pants
- Draping a large scarf over one shoulder and cinching it at the waist with a leather belt
- Wearing an unusual pin and/or earrings
- Trying short boots under pants
- Adding textured hosiery
- Belting a heavy-weight fabric blouse over a skirt or pants
- Wearing a tapestry vest or jacket
- Selecting a dual-faced watch
- Carrying a pocketed brief bag
- Wearing wire-rimmed eye frames

The key is not to overwhelm with too many unusual combinations or accessories. You can alter the look by following the guidelines for Dramatic style.

Dressing Down: Casual Styles

In an effort to meet what they perceive as the desires of their employees to relax and enjoy work, many companies are experimenting with the concept of casual business dressing. Today, two-thirds of American companies allow some form of casual dress on a regular basis. The policies are as different as the companies themselves; for instance, some companies have embraced the idea completely, while others reserve it for Fridays or the summertime. Although the concept may sound appealing, employees often find this change confusing and frustrating.

The key to successful casual dressing in the business arena is to preserve a clearly defined corporate or professional image. Without this, casual dressing may communicate the wrong message and undermine your authority and success. In some forums, weekend wear, such as jeans and tennis shoes, will be acceptable; whereas in others, merely wearing pants or a sweater in place of a blouse will be as much as can be tolerated. No matter what you choose, all garments must be fresh looking, not faded or worn-out.

To determine what is appropriate, first assess your corporate image and then ask yourself the same basic questions posed at the beginning of the Defining Your Options chapter. Despite the more relaxed nature of your attire, you will need to communicate the same basic message as when you are more formally dressed. While the Sporty style may be best for your dress down days, you can also relax the other Classics styles, that is, Traditional, Elegant, or Dramatic. Here are some suggestions:

Traditional:

Casual dressing for Traditionals is a mature form of Sporty styling in rich or neutral colors. Here the focus is on mix and match separates, fuller, longer skirts, pleated or easy-fitting pants, shirtmaker dresses, cardigans or blazers, and flat shoes. If you are a Traditional, never allow your casual look to become worn-out and faded due to excessive wear. If you borrow items from your regular Classic wardrobe for casual dressing (jacket, skirt, pants, etc.) try buying duplicates to allow for repeated wearing.

Elegant:

This is the most difficult style to convert to dress-down. A true Elegant will consider pants casual regardless of the situation and will never be caught without earrings and matching shoes and handbag. Therefore, to retain the full message behind Elegant dressing you need to stay away from most weekend wear, such as jeans, clothing with an exaggerated fit (either too loose or too tight), bright colors, or roughly textured fabrics. Keep your casual focus on matched pantsuits, sweater sets in place of a jacket and blouse, fuller skirts and smooth, fine leather flat shoes.

Dramatic:

Here is another style that can be difficult to translate from dressy to casual. By keeping the strong color contrast, firm fabrics, and extended shoulder line you can create striking casual combinations. Most outfits will start with solid-colored pants and add a contrasting jacket over a shirt matching the pants or jacket; striped shirt; dark T-shirt or turtleneck under the shirt. And bolder accessories are always worn with casual clothing (at a minimum large earrings and distinctive belt and/or scarf). Popular jackets for Dramatic casual are bomber, shirt, and cropped styles. Dresses will feature exaggerated shapes and contrasting details. Also, multi-colored flat shoes or short boots add boldness to any casual outfit.

Enhancing Your Image

Enhancing Your Image

To ensure a complete and effective image you need to master the essentials of colors and fabrics as well as understand proportions, fit, accessories, and grooming. Remember, no detail is unimportant.

Winning Fit

UNDERSTANDING YOUR FIGURE

The greatest gift you can give yourself is an appreciation for and acceptance of your body the way it is. Buying or altering clothes for the look of a custom fit allows you to consistently accentuate the positive, regardless of your shape. No matter how expensive the garment, if it doesn't fit well it will detract from your image.

As we age our body weight and proportions shift, creating changes in the way clothing fits. You will undermine your image by trying to wear tight-fitting garments. There is no better way to announce to the world you have gained weight than by wearing tight clothing. A common trap that women fall into is buying clothes a size smaller, hoping to lose weight. Unless you are clearly on the road to losing weight, this will do little more than lead to either an unflattering look or a closet of useless garments.

Another common mistake is not understanding proportions and how clothes should fit a body. This misunderstanding will invariably lead you to believe that what looks good on an ideally-proportioned store mannequin will look equally good on you. But in real life there are very few women with ideally proportioned figures. Most of us have some incongruities, whether overly long legs, short waists, or broad hips. It is for this reason that one style of jacket may look different on two women of the same height and weight. Although a standard blazer will flatter most women of standard proportions, if a woman of similar height and weight has shorter legs and fuller thighs, the identical jacket will shorten the look of her legs and accentuate the fullness of her thighs.

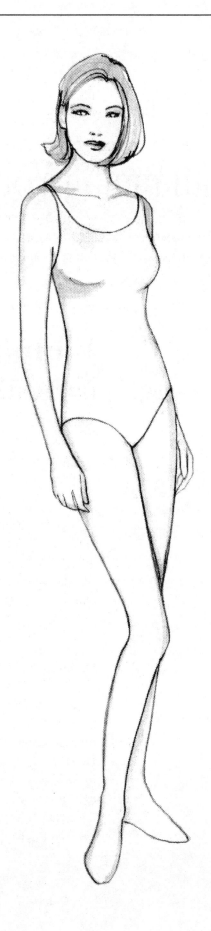

BALANCING PROPORTIONS

To properly interpret your body's dimensions you need to understand the standard body proportions, that is, both the vertical and horizontal definitions of your figure. The body is divided into four natural vertical divisions: top of head to underarms, underarms to top of the thighs, top of thighs to the middle of the knees, and middle of the knees to soles of feet. The waist should be about half way between your underarms and top of your thighs. Typically the first two divisions are combined and referred to as the torso, while the bottom two are the legs.

These natural divisions are the key to understanding which lengths of jacket, skirt, and dress are best for you. However, they are only part of the picture. To complete your understanding you must also know the horizontal definitions, the width of your shoulders, waist, and hips. In an "ideal" figure all four natural divisions are equal to one another, shoulders are at least as wide as the hips (possibly an inch or two wider) and the waist is ten to twelve inches smaller than the hips. However, in reality, very few women meet these proportions. Therefore, learning how to compensate for your differences will improve your ability to choose the right clothing regardless of your height, weight, or proportions.

You can enhance your figure by understanding the basic concepts of proportion.

Length:

Begin with the vertical proportions. The right length will make you appear taller.

Jackets:

A longer jacket (to top of thighs or lower) will make your legs appear shorter. Conversely, a shorter jacket (above the top of the thigh) will make your legs appear longer. However, a shorter woman can wear a longer jacket if it is well fitted through the body and worn with a matched slim skirt (mid-knee or shorter) in the same color.

Coats:

Coats are meant to cover all clothing with an extra two to three inches at the bottom. If you have short legs, keep the bottom portion of the coat slim. If you have longer legs, you can wear fuller coats.

Skirts and Dresses:

You can determine the proper length by considering both the length and curve of your legs. Shorter, slim skirts are best for short legs; whereas longer full skirts flatter long legs. However, if you have shorter legs you can wear a long slim, mid-calf skirt if the color of your shoes and hosiery is coordinated with the color of the hemline. Fuller ankles and calves will look slimmer with longer, fuller skirts. Also, the shape of your leg tends to determine your best length, typically, somewhere between mid-calf (either at the top or bottom of the curve of the calf) and just above the knee. Avoid hems at the fullest part of your leg.

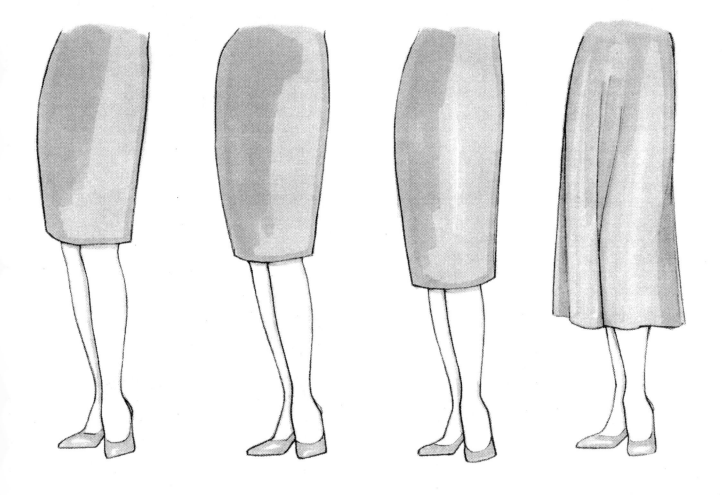

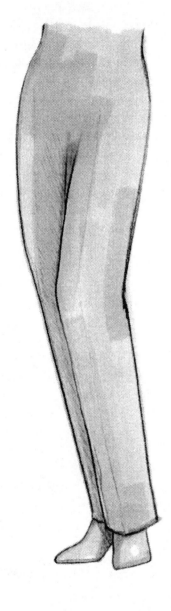

Pants:

Typically, pants should have a slight break at the top of the foot and hang longer in the back, creating a wedge effect. However, slim straight-legged pants can be hemmed to just brush the top of the foot. Cuffs should be reserved for long legs as they tend to make legs look shorter. If you choose fuller pants, the hemline should flow easily to the top of the toes, without a break.

Width:

Now that you have an appreciation for your vertical proportions, it is necessary to understand your horizontal lines and how they affect your figure.

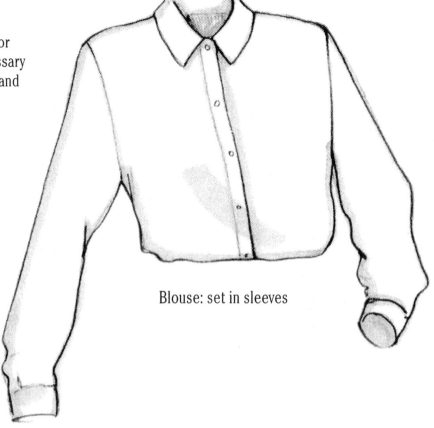

Blouse: set in sleeves

Shoulders:

As the main element of body proportion, shoulders can be adjusted to compensate for other proportion irregularities, thus visually reducing the size of the hips, decreasing a large bust, or giving the illusion of height.

Small shoulders can be given width by adding shoulder pads that extend beyond the ends of your natural shoulders. This will create balance for wider hips and de-emphasize a full bust. Other ways to create broader shoulders and a feeling of height include:

- Wide necklines, such as a boat neck, scoop, or overscaled lapels which will draw attention to the shoulders
- Set-in sleeves
- Clothing with a horizontal pattern at the shoulders
- Epaulets
- Gathers on the yoke

Broad shoulders can be minimized by V-necks, smaller lapels, drop shoulders, and halter tops.

Bust:

A small bust can be enhanced by:

- Pockets at the bust
- Horizontal lines and patterns
- Layering of clothing (e.g., sweaters or vests over shirts)
- Full, long sleeves
- Crisp, textured fabrics
- Tops bloused slightly at the waist

A large bust can be de-emphasized by:

- Eliminating pockets at the bust
- Adding an extra button or snap at the fullest point to reduce pulling when you move your arms
- Wearing more open necks, and avoiding collars and lapels
- Staying with light- to medium-weight fabrics
- Slim sleeves

Waist:

To find the right balance, you need to consider how your waist relates to your shoulders and hips. The standard proportion calls for a waist that is ten to twelve inches narrower than the hips. Also, the waist should lie half-way between the underarms and top of thighs. If your waist is closer to your underarms, you are considered short-waisted; if it is closer to the top of your thighs, you are considered long-waisted. Here are suggestions for how to compensate for these irregularities and how to de-emphasize a fuller stomach.

Short-waisted:

• Jackets and vests extending to below the hip bone

• Jackets matched to the skirt or pants to eliminate horizontal lines at the waist

• Tunic sweaters and tops

• Waist-less garments

• Narrow belts in a color matching the top

• Stitched-down pleated skirts

• Slim skirts with minimal gathers at the waist

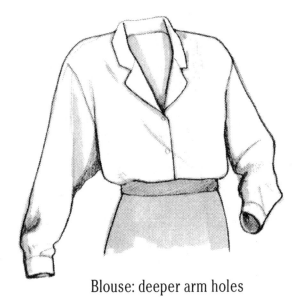

Blouse: deeper arm holes

Skirt: minimal gathers at waist

Long-waisted:

• V-neck tops

• Shorter jackets

• Jackets with a curved rather than straight hem

• Deeper arm holes in tops

• Raised waistlines or a wide belt in a color that matches the bottom

• Narrow skirts with tapered sides

• Classic straight-legged pants

• A full skirt or wider legged pants will require two-inch heels to add length to the leg

• Hosiery and shoes in colors to match the skirt, pants, or dress

• A slight heel of at least one inch

Full-stomached:

- Soft pleats at the waist
- Loose belts
- Hard finish fabrics
- Side slash pockets
- Tunic tops
- Stitched-down pleated skirts
- Tapered sleeves
- Front-zippered pants

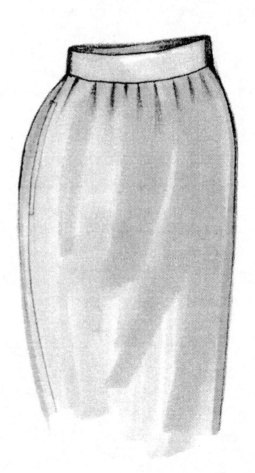

Hips:

Remember that your hips need to be balanced with your shoulders. Here are some suggestions on how to decrease or increase the size of your hips.

Large hips:

- Slim skirts with tucks at the front and back rather than at the sides
- Stitched-down pleated skirts
- Loose-fitting or dropped belts
- A longer skirt (more than two inches below the knee)
- Jackets that hit just below the fullest part of the hips and have slight definition at the waist
- Tapered sleeves
- Dark-colored skirts and pants
- Avoid bulky shoulder bags that draw attention to the hips

Small hips:

- Fuller skirts
- Bulkier fabrics
- Generous, pleated pants
- Longer jackets with a full skirt
- A peplum jacket if you also have a slim waist

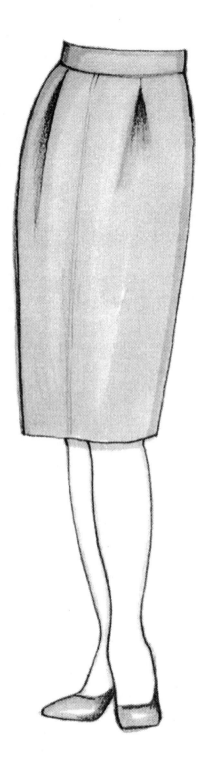

Thighs:

To minimize full thighs, look for clothing with the following characteristics:

- Front pleats on skirts or pants
- Skirts that fall just below the knee or longer
- Straight-legged pleated pants, no cuffs
- Front or back zippers

A good fit

GETTING A GOOD FIT

A good fit allows you freedom of movement without compromising the look of the garment; the clothing should fall evenly without pulling, buckling, gapping, or straining.

- Shoulders extend one inch beyond your natural shoulder edge

- Collars and lapels lay flat without wrinkling or gapping

- Jackets end either above or below the fullest place on the hips

- Sleeves fall to just below the wrist bone on the top of the hand (be sure to check each sleeve since arm length may differ)

- Buttons remain closed and the garment does not show strain across the bust

- Waistband sits on the natural waistline and is loose enough to allow for expansion (you should be able to insert two fingers comfortably)

- Allow one-half inch of fabric on each side of the hips so you can sit down without the garment riding up and pockets pulling apart

Undergarments:

What you wear underneath is important to how you look on the outside. Aim for a smooth look by selecting briefs that fit loosely, so the elastic never cuts into the legs or hips to create "panty lines." A properly fitted bra is critical for avoiding bulges and concealing nipples. Also, positioning of the breast by the bra is important. The bust is half way between the shoulders and waist — too high and you look artificial; too low and you look matronly. Be highly critical of a bra and how it makes you look before buying it.

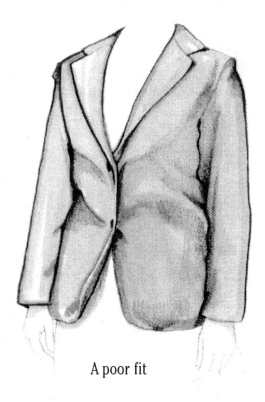

A poor fit

Alterations:

For most women the best bet is to have ready-made garments altered because rarely do you find the right fit off the rack.

When having clothes altered, you need to be realistic. Helena Chenn, designer and dressmaker of H.C. Designs, Reno, Nevada, suggests:

- Garments can be changed one size: for example, a 10 to a 12 or 12 to a 10

- Delicate fabrics may not be expandable because doing so might reveal needle marks in the fabric

- The easiest parts to alter are waists, side seams, and pant rise, depending upon the seam allowance

- Lapels can be narrowed, but not expanded

- Shoulders can be decreased. Adding shoulder pads can be done if there is enough room in the armhole

If the dressmaker is truly talented, you will be surprised and delighted by the result.

SPECIAL SIZES

Because not all women are built alike, here are some tips for tall, petite, and plus size women.

Tall Women:

Any woman 5'7" or over is considered tall. Height gives you a more commanding presence naturally. However, for those instances when you want to take a less commanding position, try:

- Medium to light colors

- Softer fabrics and shapes

- A minimum of accessories in medium scale

- Different-colored tops and skirt or pants (such as navy and taupe)

- Low heel or flat shoes

Petite Women:

Petite women are those 5'3" or shorter. If you are in this category you can create an illusion of height with:

- Matched suits

- Perfect fit; jackets should be well defined at the shoulders and waist to anchor the shape

- Shorter skirts when wearing longer fitted jackets

- Skirts that are either tapered and short in length (mid-knee or higher) or longer in fluid fabrics that fall close to the body

- Narrow-shaped pants; however, well-fitted fuller pants in a softer fabric can also be flattering

- Accessories of medium size; earrings that tilt upward from the lobes, which will make your neck look longer

- Moderate heels with a low vamp to make legs look longer

- Hair that is short or worn close to the head to make your head look smaller, which in turn makes you look taller

Plus-Size Women:

Suzan Nanfeldt and Catherine Schuller, owners of Emerging
Visions Enterprises, are internationally recognized image
and marketing experts on the plus-size woman. They offer
larger women the following advice:

- Fair or not, the world holds the plus-size woman to a higher standard of neatness, cleanliness, and style. Unfortunately you can be labeled disorganized, slovenly, or out of control more quickly than smaller women. Because wear and tear shows faster on plus size clothes, be cautious of wrinkles, stains, fraying, and loose threads. This is especially true of shoes — keep them polished and stain-free.

- Proportion in dressing is more important than trying to look thinner.
  Avoid top- or bottom-heavy looks, and focus attention on the face with color and line.

- Vertical lines elongate and flatter you. Find them in seams, plackets,
  zippers, pleats, and stripes. Beware of horizontal lines.

- Comfort can turn to sloppy in a hurry (watch those lap wrinkles and saggy knees). Choose fabrics that wrinkle slowly and retain their shape (for example rayon or wool crepe)

- High-contrast dressing can be a powerful option, but be aware that attention is drawn to the contrast line. (A white jacket over a navy skirt will focus the eye on the bottom edge of the jacket, for instance. In this case, a longer jacket that ends below the widest part of the hips would be best.) You can modify the effects of contrast by wearing colors closer in tone or by obscuring the contrast edge with pattern or shape (as with a ruffled or soft, flowing fabric).

- Don't buy anything that hugs, binds, or clings to your body. Try instead to choose fabrics that fall away from the body. Always check the rear view — half the world sees you that way!

- The secrets are in the cut. Jackets and tunics should be on the longer side; stay with narrow waistbands if they are called for; and try to wear a skirt that is below the knee or longer.

- You are only as wide as your widest line. Taper skirts and don't wear clothes larger and bulkier than necessary.

- Foundations are critical to your wardrobe. Several perfect-fitting bras are the best investment you can make. Also, be sure to wear camisoles under blouses to smooth out lumps and bumps, and always wear a slip.

- Less is more in jewelry. Avoid necklines that close in the neck area if you have a fleshy neck or double chin. A classic pair of earrings of medium to large size will balance you out. Be cautious of too many round shapes, which may reinforce your curves.

For more information on plus size dressing, order Suzan Nanfeldt's book
Plus Style: The Plus Size Guide to Looking Great!
by calling (201) 941-1753 or faxing your request to (201) 943-4616.

Color Talks

Color is a powerful tool for communication that can strengthen your physical presence. It influences the response you get from others. For instance, a woman in a red suit may intimidate others whereas in a black suit the same woman may find others looking to her to control the situation or provide leadership. Therefore, although both colors are acceptable in a business situation, which to wear should depend on the desired effect. Dark colors have the most authority, or, when accented with lighter or bright colors, can create an even more powerful look. Middle shades (those that are neither too dark nor too light, such as slate blue or rose) are best for creating a feeling of approachability.

Well-coordinated wardrobes, other than Elegant, consist of a dark, a light, and your best red. For example, you could have black, white, and red. Or navy, taupe, and rose. Or khaki, tan, and coral. The red or warm color (red, rose, or coral in these examples) adds vitality.

Here are some basic suggestions to help you select items that are right for the situation and for your personal coloring (eyes, skin, and hair).

MAJOR COLOR GROUPINGS

There are six major color groupings for business attire: neutral, subtle, jewel, bright, pastel, and rich.

Neutral:

Colors symbolize the basic tenets of traditional dressing; neutrals convey an air of maturity and dependability. The choice of colors within this grouping includes conservative shades such as navy, gray, dark green, burgundy, tan, taupe, and camel. Black, because of its versatility, is now also considered a neutral.

Subtle:

The focus of subtle color is on prestige and formality; the more-often used shades are cream, beige, pearl gray, mauve, sea mist green, and slate blue.

Jewel:

When looking for an opportunity to stand out and take control, wear jewel tones such as garnet, emerald, fuchsia, royal, amethyst, brilliant diamond white, and onyx. The more contrast there is in your personal coloring, especially between your hair and skin (for example dark hair and light skin or vice versa), the better suited you are to jewel tones.

Bright:

Youth, spirit, and energy are emphasized by such upbeat colors as orange-red, turquoise, canary yellow, grass green, nautical blue, and crisp white. These are excellent choices for casual wear, evening wear (if the color would be too bright for daytime), and for accent pieces.

Pastel:

Quiet colors that convey a feeling of support and gentleness, pastels are powdered or very light shades of any color. They are best used as accents, for example in blouses and scarves. If you have a yellow or olive skin tone be careful selecting pastels, which do not tend to flatter, ideally limiting them to small accents.

Rich:

Solid, unpretentious, and earthy are the hallmarks of rich colors. Here you find brown, plum, rust, gold, olive, khaki, and a muted teal. These are complimentary colors for olive-skinned women and most redheads.

SPECIFIC COLOR FAMILIES

Now that you have the foundation of color theory for professional dressing, here are some guidelines on using and wearing specific color families.

Blues:

It is rare to find a professional woman who does not own at least one core piece or ensemble in navy. This wide acceptance is due to its conservative appearance and the fact that most women, regardless of skin and hair color, can wear a shade of navy. Navy is less harsh than black and gives a feeling of approachable authority. Navy's versatility also makes it a good choice for business casual dressing.

Another favorite and often-worn blue is royal. Here, your skin and hair color need to be considered, since royal works best with dramatic colorings (such as light skin and dark hair or dark skin and hair).

Lighter blues or pastel shades should be reserved for accent pieces like blouses or scarves, or as dominant colors in summertime or in warmer climates, such as the South or Midwest. Turquoise, the brightest blue, is also a great accent color but may be more appropriate in casual or vacation settings.

Blacks:

This is the power color, especially for women. Wearing black gives a sense of presence or authority. Aside from its ability to create a powerful image, its versatility makes it the cornerstone of most wardrobes. Black outfits can often go from day to evening with a simple change of accessories. Another of black's benefits is that it can be worn in any season by changing color coordination. Try black and white for summer, and black and royal or red for winter. Within the black grouping, the grays, from charcoal to dove, are timeless colors that evoke a feeling of participation rather than leadership. Gray is not for everyone, but it works exceptionally well with dramatic coloring or gray hair.

Reds:

After years of being only an accent color in men's fashion, blue-reds have become more prevalent in business dressing. Women in public office are wearing red suits and dresses more often, especially in public appearances, because it is a color that exudes confidence. Your choice of color within the red family is very important; for instance, in a conservative environment bright red may be considered too flashy.

Jewel or rich reds such as garnet and burgundy are best for fall suits and dresses. Burgundy is authoritative, but less bold and more easily worn than garnet, and far less severe than black. Most redheads can wear burgundy well but should be careful in selecting other red tones.

Although more pink than red, fuchsia is an innovative and bold choice. It is not widely accepted because its bright tone goes against the grain of traditional business dressing. Its location in the pink category has limited its application in menswear, which in turn has suppressed some of its use in women's business attire.

Browns:

Chocolate, taupe, tan, or camel are the more acceptable browns in conservative, formal business settings. Darker-skinned women should avoid medium to dark browns since they tend to make the wearer look tired and drained. Taupe, tan, beige, and camel are frequently worn for business and are often mixed with black or navy in a well-coordinated wardrobe. These are approachable colors that are neutral enough to be worn with a wide variety of other colors. If the shade of brown is too close to your skin tone, it is best to wear it further from your face, opting for a beige skirt with a navy blazer, for example, rather than an all-beige suit.

Whites:

Great for accent, white should be worn sparingly unless you choose a creamy shade. Cream and ivory are easy colors to wear and work well in most wardrobes. In selecting a white, choose one that is no brighter than your teeth, preferably a shade darker, to avoid dulling your smile. Women with dramatic coloring are well suited to white. Any woman who desires contrast in clothing but is unable to wear white can substitute her best light color (such as ivory, tan, or light blue).

Greens:

Dark greens such as forest and emerald are good alternatives for fall and winter. Olive green and khaki can be worn year-around and are considered rich colors. Various shades of teal can be worn by virtually every woman, regardless of hair and skin color.

Purples:

This color is being brought back into women's wardrobes, especially in the amethyst and plum shades. It is a good alternative color for women who like variety.

Yellows:

In business, bright yellow is best reserved for accent pieces. This color may give some skin tones a sallow appearance. Softer shades are becoming more acceptable for major pieces in place of white and beige. In casual dressing, yellow is great for adding vitality and spirit to your look.

Oranges:

Very few skin tones are enhanced by shades of orange. Rust, apricot, and salmon may work well in some wardrobes. Be sure when trying on an orange garment that you have access to natural light so you can check to be sure the color works for you.

COLOR COMBINATIONS

There are three types of color combinations: Monochromatic, contrasting, or a blending of three or more colors. Monochromatic, a favorite of Elegant styling, is dressing all in one color, either exactly matched or of varying shades. Contrasting, putting light and dark together, is the most powerful combination. Blending three analogous colors takes a great deal of skill to avoid possible conflict. Tough combinations, such as red, purple, and blue can work if you employ a print incorporating all of the colors to tie them together. Try a print jacket with a red blouse and purple skirt or a print skirt with a purple jacket and red blouse.

Occasionally you may have to wear a color that is not the best for your personal coloring. Don't despair. With a few well-placed accents you can make a color more flattering. Try:

- Wearing a blouse or scarf in a color that compliments your skin

- Using jewelry to break up the color and add lightness and brightness to the skin

- Altering makeup (eye shadow, lipstick, and blush) to go with the colors you will be wearing

If you want additional information, there are professional color consultants who can help you. Contact the Association of Image Consultants International (AICI) at 1-800-383-8831 for a referral. Or, select one of the reference books listed in the bibliography.

Fabric Counts

What separates similar garments from one another is fabric. The quality of a fabric can add or detract from a professional image. The best fabric for a particular style or design will elevate the look from average to superior, just as poor fabric can change a great look into an unflattering one. For instance, a suit of polyester gabardine rather than wool gabardine can look stiff and unnatural.

Because fabrics are worn over the body, you need to consider your body weight when selecting the weight of fabric. Lightweight fabrics such as tropical gabardine or wool crepe will slenderize a woman's figure, whereas heavier fabrics, such as velvet and wool flannel, will increase the perception of body weight. Shiny fabrics add to the perception of body weight, dull fabrics detract from it.

When you want to maximize wardrobe coordination, limit the choice of fabric to those with smooth or slightly textured surfaces, such as wool gabardine and wool crepe. However, if you want to add more variety, select a textured jacket that can be worn with many items, dresses, pants or skirts (such as a silk tweed jacket paired with wool gabardine pants or cotton jersey skirt, or a silk dress). As a professional you want to avoid fabrics that are transparent, look wrinkled and unkempt, or crease easily.

Fabric falls into one of three categories: Natural, Synthetic, or a Blend. In addition, you have Formal and Informal and Seasonless fabrics.

NATURAL:

Derived from animal and plant sources, natural fabrics include wool, silk, cotton, linen, and rayon. The great advantage of these fabrics is their ability to breathe, thus allowing the body to maintain an even temperature. They also tend to be durable and allow for years of wear.

SYNTHETICS:

Just as the name implies, these are man-made substances derived from a chemical process. This category includes polyester, manufactured rayon, acrylic, and nylon. Generally, these fabrics are easy to care for and less prone to wrinkle. One major disadvantage is that they tend to hold body heat and perspiration, which can make extended wear uncomfortable for many people.

BLENDS:

These fabrics, a combination of natural and synthetics fibers, can give you the best of both worlds: comfort and fewer wrinkles.

FORMAL AND INFORMAL:

Formal fabrics include wool, silk, jersey, and velvet because their luxury and suitability enhance suits, dresses, and evening wear. These fabrics tailor extremely well, so garments fit better. Informal fibers, such as cotton and linen, are among the most comfortable and easy to wear, and are appropriate for casual wear.

SEASONLESS FABRICS:

Wool crepe, tropical gabardine, silk crepe de chine, and cotton broadcloth can be worn year-round in most climates. Choosing such fabrics means that you can have fewer clothes and more closet space. You can augment your wardrobe with coats and sweaters to accommodate changes in temperature.

MAINTENANCE:

A good fabric has a useful life of twenty to thirty dry cleanings. For this reason don't have clothes dry-cleaned too often. Shrinkage can be a problem with cotton and wool. Therefore, before altering new garments it is best to have them cleaned to allow for shrinkage.

Accessories: Essential Details

Brenda K. Kinsel, AICI, accessory specialist, image consultant, and fashion columnist, from Fairfax, California, believes that although accessories may come last when you dress, they are by no means unimportant. By providing the finishing touches to any look, the role of accessories is as important as the clothes. If carefully selected, accessories make the difference between being dressed and being very well dressed. Some of Brenda's suggestions are included in this section to give you the best possible advice on selecting and wearing accessories.

Most businessmen have long understood the importance of accessories. They leave the house each morning with polished shoes, a business watch, a handsome belt, and a tie that, like an arrow, draws the eye up to their communication center – the face. Imagine if a man wore scuffed shoes, a worn belt and a scuba diving watch. These details would divert your attention and by the time you stopped to consider his face, you would probably be having second thoughts about doing business with him at all.

The same holds true for you. If you are lugging around a sloppy handbag, wearing shoes with scuffed heels, a plastic watch, and jangly earrings, other people will be distracted. No matter how terrific your clothes are, or how competent you are at what you do, other people's confidence in you will be lessened.

Aside from completing your visual presentation, accessories also serve to distinguish and individualize your look. When you choose accessories that relate to your primary style, you make yourself more visible and memorable. Think of Paloma Picasso, the jewelry designer. In her popular magazine print ads her Dramatic styling is highlighted by her bold, earrings and necklace. Put her in a single strand of seed pearls and pearl post earrings and she would look less distinctive.

Although the main purpose of accessories is to complete an outfit and to highlight your features, a good "accessory wardrobe" will:

- Add color and interest to solid or neutral clothing
- Extend a wardrobe by creating different looks with the same garments (going from day to evening with a change of shoes and earrings)
- Update your clothes
- Pull pieces of an outfit together, especially when wearing separates

Accessories are personal. Often you wear shoes, belts, handbags, scarves, and jewelry more frequently than a particular outfit, since they usually can be coordinated with other clothing. Therefore, make these items special. In your accessory wardrobe, choose things you really love, cherish, and enjoy putting on everyday. Accessories can be part of a collection that you acquire over time. They can be pieces that you pick up on your travels or those with sentimental value. Acquiring a solid accessory wardrobe is a smart investment that extends and expands items in your wardrobe.

CHOOSING THE RIGHT ACCESSORIES

In this section, you will learn the essential accessory details that enhance your professional presentation, plus tips on how to choose distinctive accessories.

The role of accessories is to focus attention where you want it. To draw attention to your face, concentrate on earrings, pins, scarves, and necklaces. However, if you want to emphasize your waist and legs, concentrate on shoes, hosiery, and belts. All accessories need to work in harmony with the outfit.

Shoes

Selecting Shoes:

- Always shop for quality and comfort. Ill-fitting shoes quickly sabotage an outfit

- Be vigilant about replacing shoes before they are scruffy. Buy two pairs of the same shoe if necessary

- Buy shoes at midday when your feet have fully expanded

- Have your foot measured at least once a year. Feet flatten with age, exercise, and pregnancy. Over eighty percent of women buy and wear shoes that are too small, simply to mask the size of their feet. Don't make such unnecessary sacrifices

- If your feet are two different sizes, buy for the larger and use inserts or pads to correct the fit of the other

- Solve the problem of sore feet with medically prescribed shoe inserts; they take the pressure off certain sensitive spots and provide additional support

- Be sure there is "wiggle" room in the shoe; your big toe should not touch the tip of the shoe when you are standing

- Try to eliminate gapping at the sides by placing pads under the ball of the foot

- Select shoes that have flexible uppers and no hard seams or rough lining to irritate hosiery and feet

- If possible choose suede and/or leather. These expand more easily than patent and plastic, which tend to remain rigid and may become increasingly uncomfortable as your feet change

- Allow shoes to air and regain their shape after each wearing. If at all possible, let your shoes rest for a day or more between wearings

Coordinating with other Garments

- Shoes need to match or be a shade darker than the hemline of the garment

- When wearing a light garment, darker shoes can be used if the belt on the garment is of the same tone. For example–sable brown shoes and a sable brown belt with a camel-colored suit and ivory blouse

- Look to your hair color for choices in shoes and belts. Dark brown and black hair is enhanced with black. Brunettes and redheads look great in rich brown leather. Honey blondes are striking in camel tones. Ash blondes wear taupe well. Gray hair looks best with pewter tones. Shoes that relate to your hair color are good choices when wearing hard to match muted colors, pastels, and some brights

- Multi-colored or two-toned shoes' are appropriate as long as one of the shoe colors ties to the dominant color of your outfit

- Black shoes can be coordinated with a light outfit by adding black details somewhere else in the outfit (either by changing metal jacket buttons to black or tying a pattern scarf around the neck that has black in it)

- Dressy flats can be worn with a business suit if the shoes have leather-covered heels. Stack heels or highly-textured shoes should be reserved for casual dressing

- Matte finishes in leather (including suede) coordinate well with most clothing. Suede is no longer reserved for one season but is worn year round. Shiny surfaces, such as patent leather, define small feet and are best worn under pants where only a small portion of the shoes is visible. Shiny surfaces are better with crisp summer fabrics

- Formal business attire requires closed-toe, pump style shoes. However, sling-back shoes can often be worn in warm weather and with lighter fabrics and colors

- Boots are worn with longer skirts and should allow no break between the hemline of the skirt and the boots. Short boots are best with pants

Shoes to Complement Your Legs:

- Full legs look best in high vamp shoes (where the top comes up further on the foot) with a medium-thick heel
- Slim legs look best with a low-cut vamp, and in a neutral light color close to your skin tone
- Long feet can be minimized with color combinations, such as those in "Spectators" or by adding ornaments to the vamp of the shoe
- Heel heights are determined by the length of the skirt, dress, or pants and the length of your legs. The shorter the skirt, the lower the heel; the longer the skirt, the higher the heel

Hosiery:

Hosiery is the understated coordinating element of any wardrobe. The selection of color and texture is in direct proportion to the event and outfit. Natural skin-toned hosiery is always appropriate in business dressing, whereas some color and texture can be added for casual events.

With certain outfits hosiery can pull the various elements together. Also, it can camouflage thick legs and enhance lower body contouring with control top or support panels. A newer entry into this arena is hosiery that adds padding to the rear, giving you a tighter, higher derriere. Here are general guidelines for selecting the right hosiery:

- For business choose sheer tints in neutral shades (black, gray, taupe, navy, bone, ivory, and nude)
- Hosiery coordinates with the weight of the garment and time of the year; in summer months wear lighter hosiery, in winter months darker colors
- The more formal the occasion, the sheerer the hosiery
- Bright colors and heavy textures are considered trendy and work best in creative or casual settings
    - Opaques are usually frowned upon in conservative business settings, but are great under pants for casual dressing
    - A rule of thumb: the higher the heel the sheerer the hosiery
    - Hosiery should never be darker than the hemline. For example, an ivory skirt with black shoes should have natural or ivory hosiery rather than black
    - For colorful outfits (such as reds, fuchsia, teal) stay with natural skin-toned hosiery
    - Suntan hosiery is to be avoided because it casts an unflattering orange or yellow shade on your legs

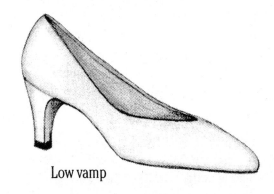

High vamp

Low vamp

Buying Hosiery:

Check the color in daylight to be sure that it is not too dark or too shiny. Also, read the sizing charts carefully to ensure the proper fit. If your height and weight put you in the gray area between sizes, choose the larger size to prevent binding and slippage.

Belts:

Even if they are barely seen, belts are important.

In selecting a belt, consider:

- Buying quality and replacing any belt before it starts to look ragged and worn

- Leather-covered buckles are the most versatile because they blend into the outfit and do not distract the eye the way a metal or ornamental buckle does

- Select a color of similar tone to your shoes

- Narrow widths are most appropriate for business (less than 2 inches)

- Coordinate the texture of the belt with the texture of the clothing fabric. Smooth belts are good with shiny, smooth fabric. Textured belts, such as crocodile or alligator (either real or simulated), are good with textured fabrics or tweeds. It may be appropriate to contrast the texture of the fabric with that of the belt, but be careful not to cause an imbalance that undermines the look

- Coordinate the color of the belt with the color of the skirt, pants, or suit. However, contrasting the color of the belt and shoes to the outfit will be appropriate for some styles, such as Dramatic or Creative

- Coordinate textures. Suede shoes and a suede belt; shiny belts go with patent leather shoes, and so on

- Consider the other accessories you will be wearing. The belt buckle should be of a similar shape, shine, and color

- If you choose to emphasize an important belt, you need to de-emphasize the other accessories

- An adjustable belt should fit with the two last holes left unused

- If you have an extra slim waist, many belts can be altered by a good shoemaker to correct the fit

- Sash belts are inappropriate for most business situations. Stay with leather, and, in some cases, metal belts with a dull finish

- For belts with Velcro® closures be sure that the closure lies flat and is fully covered. The Velcro® is not meant to be an extension piece, but rather a secure fastener

To draw attention to the waist, try:

- Shiny or bright buckles

- Colors that contrast with the main garment

To de-emphasize the waist, try:

- A belt in the same color as the garment in a matte finish with a covered buckle

- A width no greater than one inch

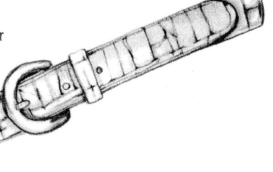

Handbags:

The right bag will accommodate your personal necessities and act as an extension of an outfit. In selecting a bag, concentrate on finding one that blends with the intended outfit. Try to limit patterned bags to solid outfits, especially where the pattern covers more than a third of the bag's surface. For most women, a solid-colored bag will be the most versatile. The color of the bag can be matched to either the shoes or the outfit. Choosing neutrals will eliminate the need for several bags. In selecting a handbag, review the style tips in the appropriate style chapter and consider the following:

- Simplicity of lines
- Structure, a blending of rounded and square shapes
- Stay away from heavy embellishments and stitching
- A handbag that blends in, not stands out
- Leather or simulated leather for maximum use
- Matte finishes, which coordinate more easily than shiny surfaces
- Size of the handbag should take its cue from your body size and shape
  - smaller bags for petites and larger bags for plus sizes
  - bags ending at the fullest part of the hips will enlarge the visual perception of that area

As with shoes, there is no excuse for worn-out handbags. Replace or revitalize worn-out bags quickly, otherwise they will detract from your overall appearance.

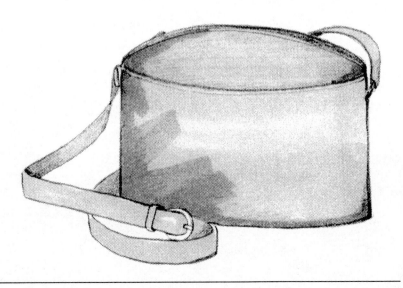

Scarves:

Scarves perform more magic than perhaps any other accessory. Like a man's tie, they add color, pattern, and variety to ensembles and bring focus to your face. They can pull together several colors in an outfit that would otherwise be fragmented. Scarves can substitute for a blouse under a suit, and change a suit from work to evening. Also, they can modify a long neck (worn as a choker or ascot) or lengthen a short neck (an oblong shape worn long and loose). Here are some ideas of how to use scarves to extend your wardrobe:

- Rectangular scarves are the easiest to wear. They can be wrapped around the neck, tied in front, or can slip inside a jacket

- Square scarves are popular but require more skill in tying and placement

- Scarves that are too short or too narrow should be avoided

- If you have thick hair or a lot of volume, you will need to purchase two of the same oblong scarves in order to look balanced. Women with thin hair need less volume in their scarves

- If the scarf is the main accessory, be sure all other details stay minimal – belt buckles are covered, shoes blend in – so there is no distraction

- If you are trying to put two or more colors together, such as an ivory blouse, tan skirt, and navy jacket, look for a scarf that incorporates all three colors

- Use a scarf to brighten the face when wearing a color that is not so flattering to you

- Be sure you have scarves in your accessory wardrobe that repeat your hair or eye color for strong impact

- Change seasons by adding lighter, brighter scarves in spring and summer, and darker scarves in fall and winter

- Scarves with luster, sequins, or metallic threads are suited to evening wear

- To quickly update classic clothing without having to purchase a new ensemble, consider adding a few new scarves each season

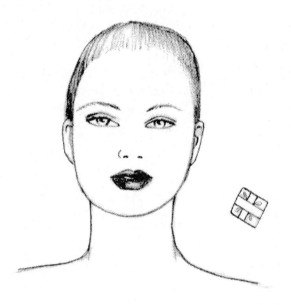

Jewelry:

The jewelry you choose to wear is very personal and needs to be selected carefully. There are two schools of thought regarding the appropriate mix of face and jewelry shapes. To highlight your face, you can repeat the shape of your face in the design of the jewelry. Conversely, if you want to de-emphasize a facial feature, select jewelry in shapes that contrast with the shape of your face (such as round earrings for a square face or angular earrings for a round face).

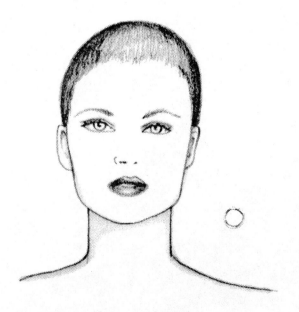

Consider color:

Not everyone wears all metal colors well. There are many metals to choose from – silver, gold, pewter, copper, and antique metals. Women with blue eyes often wear cool metals (silver and pewter) well, while women with brown eyes often look best in warm metals (gold and copper). Redheads are enhanced by burnished metals and copper. Ash blondes look great in silver and antique metals. Experiment to see what brings out the best in your personal coloring.

Consider scale:

Scale the size of jewelry to your facial features and body structure. If you are a plus-size woman with delicate features, wear large-scale jewelry with delicate details. On the other hand, if you are petite with large features, full lips and a prominent nose, you could wear larger accessories with dramatic lines.

Consider your skin texture:

If you have freckled skin, smooth and shiny surfaces may stand out like neon lights. Matte finishes, like brushed silver or gold, blend in better. If your skin is very smooth, then shiny and smooth surfaces will resonate well with your skin. A combination of shiny and matte finishes in a piece of jewelry can work for almost all skin textures.

Consider personality, energy level, and the sound of your voice:

If you have a soft voice and glide into a room like a breeze, you should wear jewelry that is similar in feeling–perhaps silver jewelry with simple, light designs. On the other hand, if you have a hearty voice, you will need to match that with some boldness in your jewelry. If you are quick to laugh and playful, whimsical or colorful jewelry, such as a strand of multi-colored beads, will complement your lighter character.

JEWELRY SPECIFICS

Earrings:

For the professional woman, earrings should be set close to the face, up on the ear. Dangling earrings are too conspicuous for most business situations, although they may be accepted in more creative settings. Some tips on selecting earrings:

- Shiny metal earrings will add a sparkle to dramatic coloring that is, high contrast between hair and skin

- Earring size should always be in proportion to the size of your head and facial features. Here are some hints for determining the proper size:

  – small faces can wear earrings up to the size of a dime

  – medium faces can wear earrings between the size of a dime and a quarter

  – large faces can wear earrings larger than the size of a quarter

- If your cheekbones are well-defined, earrings that are flat and worn closer to the head will be complementary. On the other hand, sculpted earrings with a raised dome will give the cheekbones more definition

Remember, jewelry needs to be in line with all the aspects of your outfit and image. So be sure that the styles, colors, and textures all work together.

Tips for making earrings more comfortable:

- If you tend to get headaches or ear pain from clip earrings, try adding pads to the back of the front piece and to the clip on the back

- Remove a clip earring when answering the telephone to avoid pain from dragging the receiver down on the earring

- If you are prone to allergic reactions from pierced earrings, consider posts of 14-carat gold or surgical steel

Necklaces:

The key to selecting the right necklace is to balance the length of the necklace with your neck length. Shorter necklaces decrease the length of longer necks, and longer necklaces increase the length of shorter necks. Also, you should coordinate the necklace design to the shape of your face.

- Don't forget scale; the larger your facial features, the larger the beads or width of the necklace

- If you have fullness in your hair, or a wide face, you may want to wear multi-strands in order to balance your face

- If the necklace you are wearing is strong in design, be sure the earrings take a supporting role so they do not overpower the necklace

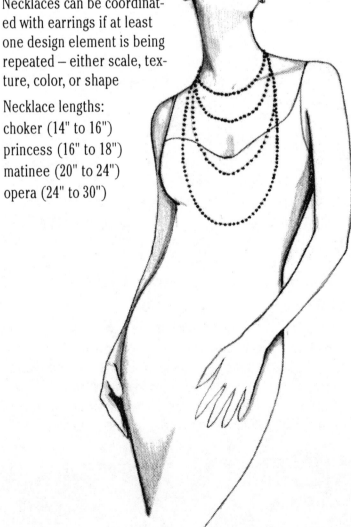

- Necklaces can be coordinated with earrings if at least one design element is being repeated – either scale, texture, color, or shape

- Necklace lengths:
  choker (14" to 16")
  princess (16" to 18")
  matinee (20" to 24")
  opera (24" to 30")

Pins:

A pin worn on the lapel or at the front of a blouse collar is a wonderful way to draw attention to the face. Relate the pin to the earrings in the same way you would a necklace, by coordinating scale, shape, color, and/or texture. Draw an imaginary line from the widest part of your face down to your lapel and center the pin from that line. If the pin is too far away from that imaginary edge of your face, it is hard to focus on you; too far inside that line and your facial features appear crowded; too far down on the lapel and it pulls the face down. Keep the pin closer to the face so the eye quickly can move from the pin to your face. Only choose a pin if you are not wearing a necklace. If you choose to wear more than one pin, go for an odd number, such as three, and arrange them in a cluster.

Bracelets:

If you enjoy bracelets, choose quiet, discreet styles for business. Wearing too many bracelets can be overwhelming and distracting. Remember, bracelets do draw attention to the hands and nails, which should be well-groomed.

Rings:

Here is a case where less is more. Try to restrict yourself to one discreet style per hand.

Watches:

You can choose metal, leather, or fabric bands. If you intend to wear the same watch with all outfits, be sure that the band color fits into the general color scheme of your wardrobe. If you have a gold or silver watch band, be sure to coordinate the metal with your other accessories. A metal band incorporating both gold and silver will blend well with most other accessories. Avoid plastic or chunky metal watches for business attire. The fit of the band should be secure but not tight. If you gain weight, replace the band, or have it professionally extended to create a more comfortable and pleasing fit.

Hair Ornaments:

These should be kept to the color of the hair so as not to overwhelm your look or detract from the other accessories. Keep the design simple.

Eye Frames:

This is the most important accessory for women who wear glasses all the time. Keep current with styles and carefully select eye frames to flatter your face and enhance your image. A friend may be needed to lend objectivity to this important task. Your eye frames should also fully coordinate with other accessories and clothing. Further, they need to fit comfortably and securely.

In choosing eye frames, aside from the shape of your face, you should consider:

• The top of the eye frame blending in with the eyebrows, to avoid the look of having two sets of eyebrows

• If frames are too small for the face, your eyes will appear too close together

• Frames that curve down on the outer corners of the eye create a tired look

• Metallic and frameless glasses are more versatile than colors

• Nonreflective coatings allow for a clear view of the eyes

• If your face is wide, the frames should extend slightly beyond the sides of the face to minimize its width and create the illusion of length

• Close-set eyes need frames with a neutral bridge and emphasis on the sidebars. Broad-set eyes need emphasis on the bridge

Grooming for Maximum Effect

Your image is not complete without good personal grooming. Hair, makeup, nails, choice of fragrance, and a warm smile are important to your effectiveness. Coreen Cordova, professional beauty style advisor and national spokesperson for the personal care and beauty division of a major corporation, offers the following recommendations for personal grooming.

HAIR

Your hair can be a major accessory. Professional dressing calls for healthy-looking clean hair cut in a moderate but fashionable style. An appropriate style is neat and easy to maintain. Color and permanents can be tricky and should be kept natural looking. Color can blend or add some contrast. Perms should be soft, not too tight, or overwhelming. The secret is to always consult with a professional stylist before making a major change.

Never overlook the need to balance your hair style with your bone structure, height, and body proportions. For instance, a petite woman will be overwhelmed by long, full hair. A plus-size woman needs volume, not necessarily length, to balance her look. If in doubt about what cut and style are most flattering for you, consult with a professional stylist. To find a good stylist, ask for a referral from women whose hair cut and styling you admire.

FACE

Successful makeup application begins with good skin care. Both skin care and makeup application should be simple and easy to accomplish every day. Makeup is meant for the enhancement of your skin and facial features, not a mask to hide behind. An appropriate makeup look should take you ten to twenty minutes. This is one area where less is best.

Skin Care Tips:

Routine is key to maintaining good skin and a healthy appearance. Everyone needs to cleanse, tone, and moisturize twice a day. To eliminate any one of these steps would compromise the condition of your skin. Using additional supplemental products, such as facial scrubs or masks, will definitely improve the overall texture and appearance of your skin regardless of your location or the time of the year. A sunscreen worn under your foundation may help prevent premature aging (reflections off of snow, water, or shiny surfaces can be just as damaging as direct sun).

Makeup:

Good makeup depends on three factors - color, placement, and blending. The choice of color is influenced by your natural skin tone, hair and eye colors, as well as the garments you wear. Placement of cosmetics depends on both the shape of your face and size of your features (here is where makeup can enhance or minimize certain areas). Blending is by far the most important step in applying makeup. There is no such thing as blending too much; natural professional makeup depends on the proper blending of everything applied to your face. If you are unfamiliar with makeup and its proper application, consult with a professional who can take the time to show you exactly how to select and apply what is best for you. If a professional is unavailable in your area, try the cosmetic specialist at a good department store.

Foundation:

Aside from hiding imperfections, foundation helps seal moisture in the skin. It is important that you select a color that perfectly matches your skin color so you do not need to apply foundation to your neck. Be sure to select one that is formulated for your skin type: oily, normal, or dry. Finish the look by applying translucent powder, which reduces the shine and keeps your foundation looking fresh for hours.

Blush:

Blush should look natural and add a hint of definition to your cheekbones. Apply blush by starting at the top front part of the ear and sweeping the color forward just below your cheekbone. The intensity of the color should diminish from start to finish, ending with a subtle bit of color in the middle of your cheek. Thus, when applied properly, you should see a hollow effect along the base of the cheekbone from your ear to the center of your cheek.

Eyes:

The most important thing is to provide definition and expression. For most women, under-eye concealer, eyeliner, and mascara are enough for most daytime events. Eyebrows should be neat and well maintained, with a shape that enhances your eyes and face. If you have dark circles or other imperfections under your eyes, select a concealer that closely matches your skin color; be certain to blend it well. If you decide to wear eyeshadow stay with neutral tones (charcoal grays, taupe, and brown) with extra color depth close to the lashline. A pencil liner softly blended around your eye will provide added focus. A touch of mascara will give an open eye effect. If you wear glasses, make sure your eye makeup is appropriate for your type of lenses. Glasses that correct distance make eyes appear smaller, therefore add a little extra emphasis to be sure your eyes are noticeable. If you wear reading glasses, your eyes will be magnified, so use less makeup (especially mascara) to prevent an overwhelming look.

Lips:

The choice of color needs to complement both your personal coloring and the color of your teeth. Colors that are too intense or frosted are inappropriate for business wear. To make the color last longer, start by applying foundation or concealer on your lips and then outlining the shape with a lip pencil in a shade that blends with the lipstick you will be wearing. Next, apply the lipstick inside the outline and blot the inner area of your lips. Remember that lipstick needs to be reapplied several times during the day.

NAILS AND HANDS

If you can take the time, a professional manicure is the best way to ensure good nail care. However, you can create a neat appearance by simply filing your nails and keeping them clean. When filing, follow the shape of your nailbed and maintain a moderate, uniform length (no longer than one-half inch). If you choose to wear polish, select a color that complements your skin tone and wardrobe (be sure it is appropriate for your working environment). Take care of any broken nails or chipped polish immediately. When in doubt, a French manicure, buffed nails, or clear polish will add emphasis and go well with all outfits. Don't forget to keep hands soft by applying hand cream daily.

FRAGRANCE

As with makeup, your fragrance should be unobtrusive and understated. Today, many items, such as hair styling products, body lotions, and deodorants carry some fragrance, so you need to be aware of the scents in your basic grooming products before adding another to the mix. Any strong scent can be overpowering and could even cause an allergic reaction in others. In recent years some companies have posted "fragrance free" zones in certain areas of the office, so be careful not to overdo the amount of fragrance during the work day.

SMILE

A pearly white smile is a definite advantage in business. The importance of healthy, attractive teeth cannot be overstated. Brushing and flossing at least twice a day is a must, along with regular visits to the dentist. Capping may be a consideration to improve the quality of your smile.

Mastering Special Situations

Mastering Special Situations

There are times in your professional life when you must step out of the office and attend an event that requires extra attention to the way you dress. Whether it be travel, appearing on television or in a photograph, addressing an audience or attending a business social event, there are some special adjustments that need to be made to ensure that you are as effective as possible.

Regional Dressing

We like to think of the United States as one homogeneous group of hard-working people. In reality, each region of the country has its own flavor, which, in combination with the others, creates our fabled melting pot. To dress properly in various regions, you need to be aware of some of the local customs. This way your look will be appropriate regardless of where your business takes you. Generally, regional styles are defined by major cities, namely, Boston, New York, Washington, D.C., Atlanta, Dallas and Houston, Chicago, Los Angeles, and San Francisco.

Here are reports from prominent image consultants on the dress variations of their respective cities.

BOSTON

Both Donna Cognac, AICI, of Donna Cognac Image Studio and Evana Maggiore, AICI, of Evana Consulting Image Marketing, point out that Boston has an intellectual image that carries over into business. This can be seen in the prominence of Traditional and Elegant styles of business dressing. Tasteful and appropriate best describe women's fashion in Boston. Proper grooming and attention to detail are more important than slick or trendy fashion. An understated, well-groomed look will do best in this environment.

When traveling to Boston, take along a neutral colored suit (navy, taupe, or black). Skirted suits are a better choice than pants. Try a smartly contrasting blouse, medium-heel to flat shoes, and minimal accessories. A strand of pearls and gold and/or pearl earrings with perhaps a scarf would add the final touch.

NEW YORK

According to Lisa Cunningham, AICI, founder of Image Management Services and, an image lecturer and consultant, New York is the fashion capital of the United States, where professional dressing features more sophistication and drama. The most often seen style types are Traditional, Elegant, and Dramatic. The garments are highly structured, and although many colors are worn, black is the most prevalent. Other prominent darker colors include purple, red, teal, burgundy, and rust. In summertime, colors turn to tan, khaki, and black in lightweight fabrics. Pantsuits are gaining prominence. Also, you find an emphasis on dramatic accessories: large earrings, more noticeable belts and scarves. New Yorkers often use accessories to personalize their style. Trends start in New York.

If you are traveling to New York, pack your best dark suits and don't forget distinctive accessories. New York can also be trendy for casual or evening.

WASHINGTON, D.C.

Angie Michaels, AICI, president of Image Resource Group, Inc., notes that Washington, D.C., is a formal city where most women favor the Dramatic and Elegant styles. Power reigns supreme, so using it properly is very important. A red suit for press conferences is common. Strong colors dominate dressing, allowing women to stand out and be noticed. Important, distinct accessories are a part of each outfit. Evening wear tends to be more formal and may require a change of clothing or the addition of a special top or accessories to your daytime clothing. Black-tie events are frequent and attended by prominent people; therefore, attention to both day and evening wear is important. Hair and makeup are conservative and understated. If you are traveling to Washington, D.C., pack a jewel-tone suit for daytime (emerald, royal, or red) and a black suit or dress for evening.

ATLANTA

Lynne Henderson, AICI, principal of CEO International and president of London Image Institute, Inc., as well as the 1995 President AICI, points out that in Atlanta you will find Elegant and Traditional suit styles with a feminine touch. The climate lends itself to a greater use of color, particularly the slightly brighter shades. Styles are marked by softer details such as more rounded shoulders, nipped waists, and lighter-weight blouses and shells under jackets. Skirts are generally worn above the knee.

Immaculate grooming, particularly well-manicured nails and flawless makeup, is very important. Hair tends to be longer and worn in softer styles, often permed.

When traveling to Atlanta, take along a suit or dress that emphasizes your feminine form, with a hemline that falls just above or to the knee, and softer blouses. Shoes are mid-heel pumps; hosiery is natural rather than colored; jewelry emphasizes quality and understatement. A separate dress to be worn with one of the suit jackets will give you extra versatility. Coat dresses would work well. Don't bring high fashion, trendy, or glamorous clothing.

DALLAS AND HOUSTON

Chris Ward, AICI, founder of Optima Image and former president of the AICI tells us that Western influence and oil wealth define fashion in Texas. The blend here is between glamour and classic dressing. Jewel and bright colors are acceptable for skirted suits in most business situations. Suit jackets are more fitted, accentuating the waist. Heels are important accessories regardless of other fashion dictates. Therefore, slim heels are worn with most outfits. Casual wear tends to reflect the area's western heritage; denim and western shirts with bolo ties are common.

Gold jewelry in larger sizes adds emphasis to business dressing. Grooming is very important. Hair is fuller, often curled, and women generally wear makeup at all times. Another important touch is well-manicured nails.

If traveling to Texas, get a good manicure and pack a suit or coat dress that emphasizes your form. Colors should be in the neutral, jewel, or bright categories, such as cream, royal, or red. Try to use larger, more expensive-looking jewelry, such as earrings and a pin, or earrings and a necklace. Also, pack something special for evening; Texans do not wear daytime fashion after dark.

CHICAGO

Nancy Penn, an image consultant with Nancy Penn Associates, tells us that Chicago women tend to be natural, healthy, and tall. The look is classic Traditional. Labels are not important, but quality is. All traditional suit colors – navy, taupe, camel, gray, and some red – are widely worn. Skirts range from above the knee to mid-calf. Matched pantsuits are beginning to make more of an appearance in professional dressing. Jewelry is kept to a minimum with emphasis on pearls and gold. More companies are incorporating dress down days, so women are switching to more mix-and-match separates.

If your business takes you to Chicago, pack a tailored suit (you can include matching pants for added versatility) with a cream blouse and low heel pumps.

LOS ANGELES

Kee Flynn, AICI, of Kee Flynn Consultations points out that a preoccupation with youth, glamour, and fitness sets the tone for dressing in Southern California, where Dramatic and Sporty styles dominate. Women tend to be slimmer and generally color their hair to hide the gray. Brighter and pastel colors are more prevalent, such as pale yellow, aqua, reds, royals, and a lot of contrast. Suits are stylish, short, and form-fitting. Pantsuits are acceptable for most business situations. It is common to see knits in place of a blouse and suits worn as two-piece dresses. Accessories are kept to a minimum. Skirts tend to be shorter than in other regions (one to two inches above the knee). Women prefer a light touch of makeup with a focus on skin care. A good haircut is very important. Flatter shoes and natural hosiery are the norm.

If you are traveling to Los Angeles, pack a colorful suit with a contrasting blouse or knit top, minimal accessories, natural hosiery, and either flat or mid- to high heel shoes.

SAN FRANCISCO

This Traditional, Elegant city pays a great deal of attention to fit. The casual air of the Silicon Valley, however, has somewhat relaxed the style of professional dressing. Long-lasting, quality clothing is more important than trends. Matched pantsuits are gaining popularity. Colors are sophisticated and tend to fall into the jewel and neutral categories. Black is widely worn due to its versatility and low-key elegance. Understatement is key.

Makeup is neat and unpretentious, with emphasis on the eyes and mouth. The large Asian community has brought San Francisco a greater variety of petite clothing and colors that work well with dark hair and lighter skin.

When traveling to San Francisco you should pack a good-quality black suit with a contrasting blouse, smart pumps, and a few pieces of good jewelry. By including a dressy top your suit can carry you from day into evening. A light coat is always a good idea because the city can see two seasons in one day.

International Business Travel

Gloria Hutter, of the San Francisco-based Gloria Hutter and Associates, an expert in business etiquette and international protocol, suggests that Traditional style works well in most parts of the world. Some countries, such as France, Italy, and Japan are more fashion and status conscious, which gives you greater latitude to be Elegant or Dramatic as well. Most women dress for dinner, so always pack a dinner dress or suit.

Here are tips for other countries and regions:

• Middle East: Clothing needs to be very conservative and modest. High necks, long sleeves, and longer hemlines are important. Pants are frowned upon and should be avoided.

• China: White is the symbol of mourning so, if you must wear any white, it should be restricted to blouses and small scarves.

• Latin America: More women are wearing bright colors and dresses under jackets. Jewelry (real or good imitation) is important and adorns any outfit.

Whether you travel in the United States or abroad, if you have any doubt about what is appropriate, contact the local Chamber of Commerce, or the United States Embassy and ask about any special requirements, especially for evening wear.

Travel and Packing Tips

The secret to stress-free traveling is to stay light and unencumbered. You can do this with proper planning and careful consideration. A bag with wheels that fits under the airline seat and a small hanging garment bag can save you time and effort by allowing you to avoid the baggage-claim areas of the airport. Also make sure you write down credit card numbers and keep them in a safe place so that you can cancel cards if they are lost or stolen.

HOW TO PACK

- Put each hanging item in a plastic cleaning bag to avoid hard wrinkles. Then you can either fold it in accordion-fashion in a standard suitcase or hang it in a garment bag. If you chose the accordion style, layer clothing to prevent wrinkling

- Carry an itemized list of what is in each of your bags for insurance purposes in case your luggage is lost or stolen

- Cover shoes with shoe mitts or socks to prevent them from getting scratched or from soiling other garments

- Roll belts, hosiery, and scarves

- Accessories should be packed in jewelry bags or similar bags to prevent them from snagging garments. Expensive or fine pieces should be carried on your person or in your handbag for added safety. However, you may feel more comfortable leaving good jewelry at home and taking better imitations or costume jewelry

WHAT TO PACK FOR A WEEK-LONG TRIP

- Begin by choosing basic pieces – jackets, skirts, and pants – in two colors, a light and a dark (for example, navy and camel or black and cream). This way you can mix and match several pieces for many day's wear

- Pack eight pieces that can be coordinated to create several outfits

    – two jackets

    – two skirts or two pants, or one of each

    – four tops of various necklines, fabrics, and colors. One of the tops can match each of the skirts or pants for a more formal look

- If the flight is relatively short, consider wearing three of the pieces on the plane, such as a jacket, pants, and top. If the weather at your destination calls for rain or low temperatures, be sure to take along an all-purpose coat, such as the ever- trusty trench coat. Also, packing clothes that can be layered will give you more flexibility if the weather changes (a thermal silk T-shirt is great for colder weather). Longer flights may require you to wear more comfortable clothing on the plane and to pack your business clothes

- Accessories should include two belts, two pairs of earrings, three or more pairs of hosiery, and two pairs of shoes. Be sure that the belts and shoes coordinate with each of the skirts or pants.

- Take scarves that can be used to transform an outfit from one look to another. This will extend your wardrobe and keep you looking fresh

- Take along a few well-selected items to convert your daytime look into appropriate evening look, such as a dressy top, glittery or dangling earrings and a special pair of shoes

- Don't forget workout clothes, you may have an opportunity to visit the local gym

- Lingerie should be flattering, but not too bulky

- Separate toiletries from other items by placing them in plastic bags or a cosmetics bag. Lotions and creams tend to expand in the thin air of airplanes and could leak. Most travelers also find it helpful to carry a small first-aid and sewing kit for little emergencies

- Take along some extra plastic bags to separate soiled clothes from other garments

- A small heating pad is comforting in a strange bed after a long trip to soothe you and make it easier to sleep

- Keep your clothes looking their best by taking along a roll of masking tape to remove lint

Television Appearances

Television is one of the most influential and widely used means of communication. During your career you may have the opportunity to appear on television many times.

Appearing on camera is an opportunity to showcase your abilities, so it is important that you are well prepared. Carefully select your clothing and accessories and take the time to apply your makeup properly. Unless you have gone through the experience before, you may be surprised how you look on camera. Although it no longer adds ten pounds as the older technology did, video does exaggerate other things, such as brightness of colors, bold patterns. and shiny jewelry. For example, extremely bright, dark, and contrasting colors bleed outside borders and create a halo or moiré effect; bold prints, stripes, checks, and polka dots look as though they are vibrating; and yellow and green give a sallow tinge to some skin tones. Your best bet is to stay with garments in the middle value and jewel tones, which tend to be the most flattering to most skin colors on camera. If you are fond of a certain color family, such as red, and find that a brighter shade doesn't work, try a subtle variation like wine or rose. Also, stay away from stark white, which tends to vibrate on camera, and instead choose a light shade of gray or pastel blue, which reads as white but doesn't vibrate.

CLOTHING

If possible, wear an appropriate jacket and waisted skirt or belt. This will enable you to attach and conceal the microphone cord and battery pack. Shape and fit of clothing are also important. Baggy, loose clothes will look sloppy. You want to look neat and trim with jackets well fitted around the collar (avoid ripples, or gapping, which occurs when collars pull away from the jacket). Be sure to take notice of how the whole outfit looks while standing, sitting and moving about, even if you may not be moving around on tape. If sitting, be sure to pull down the back of your blouse or jacket to prevent the fabric from bunching at the neck. You need to be sure that any body movements, such as raising your hand or shifting your body weight in a chair, will not disturb your look. If your legs are to be seen, be aware of skirt slits when sitting so that they don't end up showing more than you intended.

Make sure your outfit works with the set backdrop (you want to avoid blending in or creating an unflattering contrast). If you are on a television show, watch it several times to identify the colors and styles of the set. You want some contrast so you will be clearly seen, so selecting the appropriate colors for your outfit will depend on the colors of the set. For instance, if the background is beige or cream, wear royal, green, or navy blue; if it is a deep blue, wear cream or a lighter blue, apricot, or salmon. What you want to avoid is blending in with the background and losing your effectiveness.

Noisy fabrics will be "heard" on camera and can be very distracting. Also, reflections from shiny or highly textured surfaces can be hard on the eyes. Choose fabrics that are soft and have a matte finish.

ACCESSORIES

Like garments, accessories will reflect light if they are too shiny. Matte-finish gold or silver button earrings and a necklace work best. Eyeglasses with nonreflective lenses will avoid glare and distortion. Earrings should be in a size smaller than the eye so as not to detract from your face.

HAIR

Neat, carefully groomed hair either pulled back, shoulder length, or face-framing works well on camera. The key is to keep hair out of your eyes and away from your mouth so it does not detract from speaking and eye contact. Dark hair in a controlled style may be too severe and look more like a helmet than natural hair.

MAKEUP

Today most television guests are required to apply their own makeup. So, if you choose not to hire a professional cosmetician there are some rules you need to follow to ensure a flawless look. The overhead lights in television studios cast shadows on the face and will draw attention to dark circles and facial lines; so you should apply concealer carefully. A camera can pick up more subtleties than other media, therefore, do not apply makeup with a heavy hand. It is better to apply your usual amount of makeup and test it on tape. However, if you are fair-skinned, putting on more makeup may prevent a washed-out look. Bright lipstick and nail polish come across as harsh, whereas deeper shades of lipstick with blue undertones will absorb the light and create a more natural look. Translucent powder will prevent a shining face on television, so be sure to have some on hand.

Photography Sessions

Most career women will need a professional photograph for inclusion in membership directories, company brochures, press kits, and the like. It is important that the picture be current, allowing your personality and professionalism to show through. Ideally, you should replace the photograph once every two years. A glossy black and white will be easiest for reproduction in most publications. The standard size is five by seven, although four by five, or two and one-half by three and one-half, is often acceptable.

When selecting a photographer, shop around and ask all prospects to show you samples of their work before you commit. Also, be certain that you understand their fee structure and services as they tend to vary widely. Allow two to three weeks between the photo shoot and receipt of your proofs. Once you select your favorite proofs, the photographer will develop the prints according to your needs. Don't be surprised if the photographer keeps all the negatives, that is a standard practice.

A studio location is advantageous because of the ability to adjust the background, lighting, and pose to suit your needs. You need to select a background that offers contrast to the color of your clothes. Don't be afraid to stop the shoot and touch-up your makeup to ensure that there are no unnecessary lines or shadows. Remember, the goal is to look natural.

TO GET THE RIGHT PHOTOGRAPH THE FIRST TIME, TRY:

- Scheduling your appointment for mid-morning when any puffiness around your eyes has disappeared

- Applying makeup a little more heavily than usual, stressing contouring around the eyes, cheeks, and lips. A good lip pencil is essential. Given the importance of a professional photograph, you may find it an invaluable investment to hire a professional makeup artist who can apply the initial makeup and do touch-ups during the shoot

- Keeping your hair style neat and understated. Try scheduling the shoot for one to two weeks after a hair cut so the look will be more natural

- Wearing clothing that contrasts with your skin (lighter clothing with darker skin and darker clothing with lighter skin)

- Wearing a jacket or tailored dress with a simple uncluttered neckline (not too high or too low) and, if it has lapels, see that they lie flat without buckling. Be careful to avoid bold patterns

- Keeping accessories to a few select pieces, tasteful, and in a satin finish. Simple button earrings are often enough (select a size that is smaller than your eyes)

- Going without eye frames (they can cause a glare). If you want the look of eye frames, borrow a lens-less pair from an optometrist

Unless you want a serious photograph, try to look alert with bright eyes and show a smile with some teeth. Let the world see your confidence and sincerity.

Public Speaking

On stage all eyes are on you. Your clothing, as one of your props, helps to set the tone for your presentation. Your physical presence can lead the audience to tune in or tune out even before you begin to speak. Remember, you want your clothing to add to your presentation, not detract from it, because it is difficult to reverse a poor first impression.

To convey a believable image, first define the audience and your message. Then make whatever adjustments are necessary to be certain that your clothing fits the presentation, place, and time. More serious presentations (for instance, those concerning financial, legal, or governmental topics) call for a darker structured suit or dress with a contrasting blouse or scarf to reinforce your message. Conversely, for more informal situations (such as high technology or academia), try a lighter relaxed suit, dress, or coordinated separates (perhaps even a pantsuit). For more persuasive presentations, such as sales promotions or political speeches, try an eye-catching, distinctive jewel tone, such as ruby, royal, emerald, or purple in structured suits or dramatically styled dresses.

The following suggestions provide you with the basics on presenting an effective image on stage:

- Select clothing that is conservative yet distinctive, such as a red suit with a dramatic cut or asymmetrical closing

- Enhance your visibility from a distance by wearing a contrasting blouse and jacket, or a dress that contrasts with your skin color.

- If you will be moving around, select a garment that provides freedom of movement without pulling, gapping, or excessively wrinkling

- Skirt or dress hemlines should be mid-knee or longer, especially on an elevated platform where some of the audience may be looking up at you

- Develop a signature with either accessories or clothing. Try a colorful scarf, conversational pin, unique cut of the garments, or use of color

- Create a more polished look by wearing pumps with a moderate heel, especially in a formal or conservative setting

- Try to wear hosiery in natural or sheer tints

- Select earrings no larger than your eyes to prevent distraction

- Be sure your eye frames have nonreflective lenses

- Wear understated makeup for a smaller group and more exaggerated for a larger group (100 or more, where the light and distance may make you look washed-out to those in the back of the room)

OTHER VALUABLE TIPS:

- Whenever possible, check on the background color before going to the location to be sure you have the proper contrast and balance of colors. If you feel the background is inappropriate, ask if there is a screen or other back drop that can be used during your presentation

- If you will be using a clip-on microphone, be sure your outfit has a lapel for the clip and a place to attach the microphone pack (such as a belt or waistband)

- Be prepared to take your clothes with you and change before you go on stage. Impeccable grooming and wrinkle-free dressing are a must

Public speaking is one of the best ways to promote your business. If you give more than two presentations a month, you may want to have certain designated outfits that can be worn exclusively for these engagements. By doing this you always have something appropriate to wear, even if you get a last-minute call.

Job Interviews

Demonstrate your expertise and credibility by learning as much as possible about the company or position before the interview. This information can be obtained by interviewing company employees, visiting the offices, or by requesting the most recent annual report.

What does the office look like? How do the employees dress? Is the office contemporary, sleek and high tech or traditional with antiques and oriental rugs? Is it located in an urban or rural area? You need to know if the company is formal or informal so you can dress as if you already have the job. Be careful not to dress less formally than the interviewer. It is better to err on the side of formality than to be too relaxed or casual.

To reduce some of the stress in an interview, arrive fifteen to twenty minutes early and do a detailed check of your total appearance: hair, makeup, and clothing (make sure lining does not show). Since interviews can last for hours and you may not have many opportunities to refresh your look, hair and makeup need to be easy and uncomplicated. Avoid perfume, for many people have allergies to various fragrances. Well-manicured nails of moderate length are a must.

TIPS ON DRESSING FOR YOUR INTERVIEW:

Clothing

- Although pants are gaining greater acceptance, it is still advisable to wear a skirted suit, dress, or coordinated separates in a moderate length

- The choice of color will depend on the degree of formality and the season. If you prefer darker colors, remember that they tend to communicate more power, so lighter fabric may be best to understate the power message. Medium colors, like taupe, camel, or slate blue send a message of approachability and work well with heavier fabrics

- More creative fields, such as marketing, advertising, or public relations are more open to richer or brighter colors, such as olive and fuchsia

Accessories

- Jewelry should have a matte-finish, secured (that is not dangling or jiggly), and should consist of few pieces. Try to limit earrings to a single pair even if you have multiple holes in each ear. Also, avoid wearing more than one ring on each hand

- Shoes of medium height with an enclosed toe and heel. Pumps work better than sling-backs

- Hosiery in natural colors or sheer tints

- Handbags should be moderate and unobtrusive. If you need additional room for documents or other material, carry a separate briefcase. Whenever you carry both a briefcase and handbag, keep the handbag small in scale

If you do not have a complete professional wardrobe, invest in two interview suits, one in a darker color and another in a medium color, with at least two tops for each and all coordinated accessories. These items will become the starting point for your wardrobe once you get the job.

Social Functions

Every professional attends a variety of business social functions during the year, whether an office party, conference dinner dance, or cocktail reception for important clients. What you wear to these events can be challenging. You want to look special, but also have an air of professionalism.

Your image always needs to reflect you and your company. The mistake many women make is to have two different personalities, conservative business and daring evening. You want to avoid garments that are too outrageous or alluring, staying instead with tasteful dinner dresses, dressier suits, and pantsuits. Many businesses continue to discuss business even during a social function.

Generally, after-five refers to business attire slightly altered for evening by adding higher heeled shoes, drop earrings and freshening your makeup and hair. Occasionally you may prefer to wear dressier clothing, substituting a colorful dressier top and a distinct belt and shoes. Dinner dresses, suits, or dressy pantsuits are appropriate for most formal occasions that are labeled black tie. One suggestion is a basic black dinner dress in wool crepe with a modest scoop neckline worn with a slightly fitted jacket and expensive-looking jewelry. You can substitute any dark color for black. Hemlines can be longer for more formal occasions. If in doubt as to what is appropriate, contact the hostess and ask what she will be wearing, and take your cue from her.

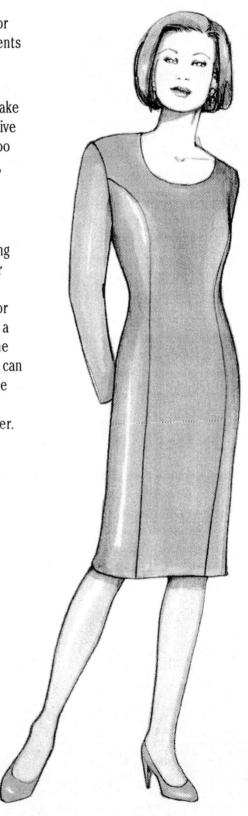

Achieving an Effective Wardrobe

Achieving an Effective Wardrobe

Once you have successfully identified which style you want and need in your wardrobe, the next step is to develop a plan of action. Start by taking inventory of your current wardrobe and deciding what works and what doesn't. As you do so, keep in mind that there are two professional services that can be invaluable: a good dressmaker and a reliable dry cleaner. Without these professionals, you may end up spending time, money, and effort needlessly. A good seamstress can keep favorites fitting just right or allow you to pick up good values and have them tailored to look like custom-made clothing. Likewise, a good dry cleaner will allow you years of wear by not unnecessarily damaging the garments with harsh chemicals and by properly pressing each piece.

Analyzing Your Wardrobe

When you open your closet door what do you see? If you are like most women, you see a hodgepodge of years of accumulation mixed with some sentiment. Women generally wear only 10 percent of their wardrobe on a regular basis; the remainder simply takes up space. A disorganized closet can make successful dressing difficult or sometimes downright impossible by not allowing you easy access to all the elements you need to create a particular look. Once organized, you also gain the added benefits of time, simplicity, and possibly cost savings that will benefit you for years to come. So you ask, where do I begin? Your first priority is taking an inventory of what you own and deciding whether or not it works for your image. Begin by putting each item into one of the following categories.

- **Favorites:** Any item that is comfortable and makes you feel good

- **Poor Fits:** Your body has changed, but the item hasn't. However, if it did fit properly it would be a favorite or core piece

- **Worn Out:** A piece that was such a favorite that it has outlived its usefulness; the fabric is thinning, stretched, shiny from wear, or falling apart

- **Outdated:** Your body may be the same, but the times have changed and you may not live long enough to see the item come back into fashion

- **Hangers On:** Items you know you don't need or want, but keep for sentimental reasons or out of a feeling of guilt (because it was a gift or a costly mistake)

- **Core Pieces:** These are the workhorses, the items that form the foundation of your wardrobe. They generally look good, but do not necessarily fit the favorite category

Your goal is to have a wardrobe of favorites and core pieces that fit, are comfortable, and are appropriate for your image and lifestyle.

Next, try on all the items that ended up in the favorite, core piece, and poor fit categories to determine if they still work or can be revitalized. All items in the worn out, outdated, and hangers on should be put in a discard pile. Try on each piece, or, if several pieces are meant to be worn together, try them on as an ensemble. Check the look and fit of the piece or ensemble from all angles, including the back. Ideally, you should check yourself in a three-way mirror; however, if you don't have access to one try combining a hand-held and full-length mirror to help you catch every angle. Some women find it fun to invite a friend over who will provide honest input, which can make the task more enjoyable. Either way, you need to be prepared for the possibility that some favorites may no longer work or that certain pieces cannot be salvaged.

Fit is, as stated often in this book, one of the most important elements of any style type. So, when you're trying on various items, be sure to ask yourself: How does it fit? If the answer is not well, can it be revitalized, repaired, or altered to become more useful? These are the types of questions that may require input from someone else; if you're doing the assessment yourself and have any doubts, take the item to an alterations expert. Once you have established what works, what needs help, and what to discard, you are almost ready to develop a strategy for building your new wardrobe.

First, however, discard items now, rather than waiting – you may lose your nerve. Separate the discards into those that may be given away (to family, friends, or charity), and those that can be sold at a consignment shop. Remember to check with your accountant to see how much of a tax deduction you can take for donations to a qualified charity.

For those items requiring help, such as cleaning, pressing, or alterations, make a plan to do whatever is necessary within the next thirty days. Procrastination may lead to inaction, and the clutter may return, undoing all the good work you have done thus far.

Organizing Your Closet

Now that you have weeded your closet of unnecessary clutter, it's time to focus on organizing what remains. This will make it easier to introduce new items. Group items by type, hanging them in the following order.

Suits: Arrange these pieces based on color, keeping color families together, moving from darkest to lightest or vice versa. For instance, deep navy to royal to turquoise then light blue, or pale gray to charcoal to midnight black. Use this same idea in structuring the entire suit category, by perhaps starting with the lightest color grouping, whites or yellows, and moving across the spectrum to the darker color families, such as blues and blacks. This will give you a better perspective on what you own and what can be coordinated.

Jackets: Follow the same color strategy used with suits and add jacket length as another variable. So not only will color families be grouped together, but within the grouping you will hang jackets from shortest to longest or vice versa.

Tops: Again, color is important, but here it is best to separate items based on sleeve length. The progression goes from sleeveless to long sleeve or vice versa. If your desired style calls for more knits, which should not be hung in a closet, place them in drawers close to the closet for easy and stress-free dressing.

Skirts or pants: Group skirts and pants separately. Skirts are hung according to length, preferably short to long. Pants may be hung lengthwise or folded over a large rod hanger.

Dresses: Hang by color or occasion – from daytime to after-five within color families. If you have dresses that can be worn with a jacket, it may help to hang them nearer the jackets but still within the category.

Once the new foundation of your wardrobe has been properly organized, it is time to determine what is needed to complete it. Here are some guidelines.

1. If you wear suits you may have the option, depending on the style of the jacket, to wear them as two-piece dresses. If you find that you need to wear tops, see rule 3 below.

2. Jackets need at least one coordinating piece, either a dress, skirt, or pants. However, if the jacket is versatile you can maximize its usefulness by combining it with numerous skirts or pants, and dresses. Here, the key is to identify the style and color of each jacket so you can select appropriate additions whenever you need them.

3. Tops: The rule of thumb is that you have at least two tops per bottom; one top should match the bottom to create a dressy look and the other should match each jacket so the combination can be worn with numerous skirts or pants. This matching allows you to create outfits with minimal problems.

4. Skirts or pants: Here the focus should be on having a few pieces in more neutral colors to simplify coordination. Certain style types, such as Elegant, may need a bottom to match every top and jacket, whereas a Sporty look may require fewer skirts or pants to coordinate with a number of tops and jackets.

5. Dresses: These items need to be coordinated with over garments. Take inventory of coats as well as jackets to ensure the completeness of your look. A coat will generally go well with all dresses; however, a jacket may be an option for certain dresses, especially those with defined waists.

ACCESSORIES

Now that the main clothing items have been categorized and organized, and you have identified which new pieces are needed, it is time to check how your accessories fit your newly defined wardrobe.

Shoes: Do you have at least one pair that is comfortable and in good shape that coordinates with a variety of outfits? You will need two pairs of shoes in your basic, neutral colors, one flat and the other with a heel. Basic colors include black, navy, taupe, gray, and perhaps brown. If you enjoy shoes, you may choose to purchase other colors and styles, including two-tone and textured shoes. It is important to buy shoes that are comfortable.

Hosiery: Coordinate the color with your shoes unless the color is bright, or unusual. For example, red hosiery is not likely to work well with red shoes, and white hosiery, although appropriate for white shoes, may make your legs look heavy. It is always appropriate to wear hosiery in a tint close to your natural skin tone.

Tights are generally inappropriate for business attire; however, they may work with a Sporty look, especially when they are worn under pants.

Handbags: The biggest problem is finding a bag that is neither too casual nor too dressy so that it can be used with many outfits. Therefore, review your style category and discard bags that are inappropriate. At a minimum, you need a bag for daytime and one for formal evening. As you build your wardrobe, additional bags can be purchased but may not be necessary.

Belts: These are needed to finish the look for every bottom where the waist is visible. Check your old belts for signs of wear, such as raveling, fraying, tarnishing, and stretching. Also, do not ignore ill-fitting belts. If a belt cannot be extended with additional holes or made to fit by other means, discard it.

Jewelry: At this point you will find that some jewelry no longer goes well with your wardrobe or that you are missing necessary pieces. To get a basic selection, be sure to focus on earrings first, then move on to necklaces, pins, bracelets, and other pieces.

Preparing an Action Plan

Congratulations on getting yourself and your wardrobe organized! Now you are ready to develop a plan to ensure stress-free shopping. Start by writing a list of necessary and desirable items. Be specific, listing such details as color, style, fabric, and any coordinates in your core wardrobe. The list can be used for immediate shopping or broken down into components for several smaller shopping trips over a period of time.

Review the specifics of the appropriate style before completing your plan to be sure that you are working on a list that will truly develop an efficient, comfortable, and stylish wardrobe. You need to be sure your plan addresses all your wardrobe needs, including professional, casual, and evening wear.

Make sure your plan ties together the several keys to successful shopping; namely, it must be specific about what you need, including how much you are willing to pay for each item, and how soon you need it.

Developing a Realistic Budget

Depending on your particular needs, there are a few basic rules to ensure that your wardrobe budget is appropriate.

First, assess how the dollars should be spent. If you spend fifty percent of your time working, you should invest fifty percent or more of your wardrobe budget on items for work. There are also variables to consider such as your feelings toward clothes. Are you someone who puts a great deal of thought into what you wear each day, or do you prefer more of a uniform look where you dress within limited combinations? If you wear a Dramatic or Elegant style, the need for ensemble dressing will require a sizable initial investment and annual updates. Traditional and Sporty looks can manage with a minimum investment in core pieces that can be mixed and matched to increase the number of outfits.

Next, ask how many items you need to complete your wardrobe. If you are starting from scratch, you need to make a commitment to purchase enough to get by. As funds become available, you can purchase additional items until your wardrobe is complete. For women with more established wardrobes, the timing of the purchases may not be as important. It has been suggested that one month's net salary per year should meet your wardrobe needs. This takes into account the quality and number of items for every income.

Check the cost versus benefit of your clothing selections: When shopping, don't get hung up on sticker shock until you have had an opportunity to assess the durability of the item. For example, a suit may carry a $400 price tag and cost $8 for each dry cleaning. If you wear that suit once a week for one year, and have it dry-cleaned four times during the year, the suits real cost to you is less than $9 per wearing. The cost per day declines the longer you wear the suit; remember, good fabrics properly maintained can give you years of wear. To put it in perspective, most people working in a metropolitan area spend $5 to $10 per day on lunch at cafes or restaurants. Therefore, if your clothing is worn for a couple of years, you are actually spending about the same amount on good-quality clothing as you are on your daily lunches. So, if you want a better wardrobe, bring your lunch from home!

Adjust the timing of purchases to coincide with financial resources. If you find yourself with a long list of needed items but do not have the funds to buy everything at once, consider developing a time line to match purchases to your budget. Here the key is to set priorities; the most important items are purchased first and others are put off until later, perhaps allowing for sales at your favorite stores. Try to avoid impulse buying or overdoing it by charging everything - only to discover later that the interest on your charge account could have purchased another outfit.

Finally, to get the most for your money, clothing needs to be flexible; you should be able to create numerous outfits by coordinating garments and accessories (unless you are going for an Elegant style). Also, stay with clothing in timeless styles to allow for years of wearing.

Cheaper is not necessarily better. What is important is how much wear you get from a garment and how good it will look over time. Think of the times you have purchased a "bargain" and watched it fall apart after a few months, only to find yourself replacing it with yet another "bargain." By constantly replacing pieces you never establish a true base wardrobe and end up spending more money than originally planned.

If you are really strapped for cash and find it difficult to save money for each major purchase, you may want to consider shopping at store sales. This way you can get better items at lower cost.

DRESSMAKERS

If you find shopping difficult or fruitless, you may enjoy the benefits of a dressmaker. Here is an opportunity to get exactly what you want in a custom fit, for a price that may actually come close to or be less than what you would pay at a popular department or specialty store. The key to success with a dressmaker is finding one who is dependable, capable, and within your price range.

No-Nonsense Shopping

No-Nonsense Shopping
Successful Shopping Strategies

Shopping can be time-consuming and frustrating. However, time spent developing a strategy will reduce stress and possibly save money.

WHERE TO SHOP

In deciding where to shop, in addition to which labels you prefer, you should consider:

- How much service do you need or want? Small stores tend to offer an intimate atmosphere as well as more personal service, but the selection may be limited. If you shop at a large store, one benefit is the ability to request an item from another store location if you can't find what you want in your size. To shop at a discount store where service may be limited, you need plenty of time and the ability to accept the fact that you may not find exactly what you are looking for. Again, keep in mind that compromising may be financially unsound

- The store's return policy. Be sure to check which limitations apply to your ability to return an item, such as number of days from date of purchase, whether the garments must have original tags attached, and whether you receive store credit or full cash refunds. If the item you are returning is a one-time purchase in a store you do not frequent, the store credit may turn out to be your loss. Be cautious when shopping at a discount store where returns can be very restricted.

WHEN TO SHOP

The best time to shop is at the beginning of each season when the selection of sizes and styles is greatest. This is approximately each February through May for spring and summer and August through Thanksgiving for fall and winter. If you wait for the sales late in each season, the reduced prices may not compensate for the lack of selection. You may also spend too much time looking for what you need, if, in fact, you can find it. Try not to shop when you are extremely stressed or hurried because you may end up compromising on a piece that is not really appropriate. Buyer's remorse is all too frequent for hurried shoppers.

HOW TO SHOP

Shop alone for maximum efficiency. Generally, if you take someone along, you lose your concentration and can be persuaded to purchase inappropriate or unnecessary items. However, sometimes a friend or companion can offer valuable feedback.

Bring along your written plan to mitigate the risk of impulse buying or buying the wrong thing. Develop sales resistance to prevent being talked into buying something inappropriate or costly, and see how far the available funds can go.

Buy in groupings or units to ensure full coordination. Units are a well-edited group of clothing and accessories purchased at the same time, typically one jacket, two bottoms (skirt and/or pants), three tops, two pairs of shoes, and at least one piece of jewelry. To avoid "orphans" or costly mistakes, plan to buy a jacket or suit first, then the appropriate skirts or pants, tops, and accessories.

Develop color themes, focusing on two or three main color groupings that can be mixed or matched for easy wardrobe management. Start with a light color, such as white or off-white, tan, taupe, camel, or pale yellow, and a dark color, such as black, navy, olive, or brown, then coordinate the chosen colors with a warm color (your best red) such as apricot, coral, rose, red, fuchsia, or burgundy. The actual selection will depend not only on your skin tone but on your style preferences as well.

Shop in better ready-to-wear departments or specialty stores because the full line of coordinates are available, and it is much easier to assemble a complete look. While you are shopping, it is best to avoid buying items that do not fit today in the hope they will fit tomorrow; instead, buy with an eye toward the garment's ability to be altered if your body changes (check to see if the garment can be expanded and reduced without much notice or damage to the design or fabric). For instance, fragile fabrics such as silk cannot be lengthened or expanded easily because needle marks will show in the fabric.

Ask yourself, based on where and how often you expect to wear the item, if the fabric will hold up to numerous cleanings. Easily wrinkled fabrics are high maintenance and need to be carefully considered.

Before approaching the cash register be sure to check the item for flaws or problems with every aspect of fabric and construction. Some commonly found problems include:

- Edges and corners, especially on lapels and collars, that do not lie flat
- Zippers that may show stitching or uneven puckers
- Mismatched or uneven hemlines
- Mismatched stripes or plaids
- Loose threads on buttons, seams, and hems

In checking the fit of new items, ask yourself whether or not you have the proper foundation garments. All-in-one types (bra and panty with or without slimming panels) keep a trim line in sweaters and slim-fitting garments; slightly padded bras under sheer fabric or a camisole can finish a particular look; and slips, if necessary, should match or be slightly shorter than the length of the outer garment to eliminate exposed slip hemlines. Remember, if the foundation is not right, the look will not be effective.

Once the purchase is made, keep the receipts long enough to allow you the opportunity, if necessary, to return the garment. Write a brief description of the item on the receipt to be sure you have the right information. Some people find it useful to keep all receipts for a year, totaling their purchases to prove value in case of loss due to theft, fire, water, or some other insurable occurrence. In dealing with an insurance company claims representative, the more proof of value you have, the more you are likely to recover your money.

FINDING HELP:
PERSONAL SHOPPING CONSULTANTS

If you find shopping tedious or simply do not have the time or patience, you may be a good candidate for a personal shopping consultant. There are generally two .categories of professional personal shopping consultants: in-store and independent. The advantages of using consultants are:

- They are experts who can show you how to coordinate, accessorize, and update your wardrobe

- They do all the leg work; selecting the best items for you and exchanging styles and sizes while you are trying on your new clothes

- They keep an inventory of your new purchases for reference when you shop in the future

- A consultant can also make arrangements for your purchases to be sent to your home or office

Before selecting the services of a consultant, consider the benefits of the two main types. An in-store consultant's services are generally provided free of charge, and the consultant selects items for your wardrobe from what that particular store has to offer. Since an independent consultant has no ties to any particular store, he or she can use the wealth of the entire shopping area. An independent can also provide extensive service by doing in-home evaluations of your wardrobe, inventory management, and coordination follow-up. The fee for these services varies by the experience of the consultant and the region of the country. It is best to interview a consultant and develop a good rapport and understanding of the available services and fees.

Therefore, to find a consultant, you can either go to a major department or specialty store, or, to find an independent consultant in your area, contact the Association of Image Consultants International, AICI, in Washington, D.C. at 1-800-383-8831. In the San Francisco Bay Area contact Image Development and Management, Inc. at 415-258-0285. Independent consultants who are members of AICI must meet high professional standards. Remember, this is a highly personal service, so you should check the prospective consultant's qualifications and references prior to the first appointment. Think of the process the way you would if you were selecting an interior designer or real estate agent. You may have to interview several consultants to find the individual who is right for you.

Doubling Your Investment

Doubling Your Investment

Purchasing all the right pieces is the beginning of what will be a long and satisfying relationship between you and your wardrobe. To secure the long life of each garment, to "double your investment," there are some basic rules to live by.

Safekeeping

Clothing must be carefully stored.

Hangers: Never, never, never use wire hangers. They leave shoulder creases and provide no support for clothing. If you have any, return them to your local dry cleaners for recycling. A much better choice is one of the following.

Plastic tubular hangers: This type is the most versatile and can be used for virtually any type of garment or fabric.

Store hangers: These tend to be of medium-quality plastic that may break after repeated use or if the garment is too heavy. Often you have to request the hangers at the time of purchase or the store will reuse them. If you do not have a ready inventory of plastic tubular hangers, the store hanger is a good alternative until the tubulars are purchased.

Wooden coat or suit hangers: Wooden hangers are very sturdy and are often found supporting men's garments.

Padded hangers: Although they are nice to look at, padded hangers do not offer the benefits of plastic tubular hangers.

Pant or skirt clip hanger: Although great for preventing creases, the important thing is to use clip hangers correctly; that is, if you want to use them for delicate or highly textured fabric, be sure to use small pieces of heavy fabric between the clip and the garment to prevent damage.

Prevent Overcrowding: After you have selected the proper hangers, be sure to preserve the garment by hanging it loosely in the closet; overcrowding can cause closet wrinkles and make it harder to detect moths. For those of you who may not have much closet space, another alternative is to hang two rods in the closet and place certain items on the upper rack and others on the lower rack. Keep one area for longer items such as coats and dresses.

Knits: It is not necessary to hang all clothing. Knits are folded to prevent the distortion that can occur when they are hung in a regular fashion on a standard hanger. Despite what your mother may have told you, the best way to fold a sweater or knit top is to first fold the garment in half by drawing the bottom up to the top, and then place the sleeves across the folded garment. When done correctly, it will look like someone is hugging the garment. For dresses, follow the same general idea but make the initial fold in quarters or thirds to reduce stress on the fabric. To avoid pulling folded pieces apart when selecting an item from a small stack, separate each piece with tissue, cardboard, or similar material. Then, when you remove items from the middle or bottom of the pile, you will not disturb the item above.

Moth proofing: This is a must if temperatures are 50 degrees or more, because your closet will become susceptible to moth larvae. Although you can use traditional mothballs, the smell may be unappealing. Alternatives include herbal mothballs, which are sold in various natural or health food stores, or (for women who do not mind making a more substantial investment), you can have your closet lined with cedar. If you choose cedar, there is no guarantee that larvae will be fully eradicated; so, additional remedies may still be necessary. Cedar is most effective when re-sanded once a year.

Light: Often women tend to overlook the impact of light on clothing. It is best to keep closets dark or dimly lit, using direct or overhead light only when selecting or returning items. Constant exposure to light may cause yellowing and fading, especially with more delicate fabrics, such as silk. For this reason we discourage skylights in closets unless there is an ultraviolet shield on the window or a cloth covering on the garments.

Storing Accessories: Pay particular attention to small accessories and hosiery, for these are the items most likely to be lost or damaged.

Shoes: Any type of storage that separates shoes so they do not rub against one another is acceptable. If you have little room, there are a variety of shoe caddies that come in all shapes and sizes. Here, your space and personal preferences are what is important in selecting the right system. Another option is to use the original shoe boxes and place identification labels on one end to aid in quick selection (just poke a few holes in the boxes to allow air in to prevent mildew). You can prolong the life of good shoes by inserting well-fitted wooden shoe trees between wearings.

Hosiery: Keep items together, separated by color. The container should be free of all rough surfaces that may snag or pull. Unopened packages can be arranged by color in a conventional plastic sweater box. Keep one hosiery package for each color or type of hosiery so you have the information available when you want to reorder or purchase new pairs.

Belts: If you have room on your closet wall, you may consider using hooks or a similar type of organizer upon which to hang each belt. However, for most women this is not an option, so the next best choice is to carefully roll and place the belts in a large plastic box or drawer. Be sure to roll them so that the buckles face in to prevent scratching and other damage.

Scarves: Because most scarves are made of delicate fabric, it is best to fold them as you would a knit garment. Be careful if you choose to organize them on a multi-clip hanger; put a piece of heavy material between the scarf and clip to prevent damage. Also, it is very important to avoid overcrowding because scarves can wrinkle easily.

Jewelry: The two cardinal rules are to keep pieces separate to prevent damage and to store all items in such a way that they can be easily recognized and quickly accessed.

The selection of a jewelry organizer depends on several factors including the quality of the pieces and space availability. Some lower cost alternatives are silverware or business drawer organizer trays, which can be stacked if you have a lot to store.

Maintaining Wardrobe Vitality

No clothing will look good if it is improperly maintained. When fabric is not cared for it can look worn before its time. Proper maintenance can be both inexpensive and simple.

Cleaning: To revive garments between dry cleanings, try a light brushing with the special clothing brushes you can purchase in the men's department or notions department of a major store. Also, a simple pressing may be enough between cleanings, but again, caution is required to avoid overtaxing the fabric.

Rest and air clothing between wearings. This allows the garment to regain its shape and eliminates wrinkles and odors.

Before dressing, be sure to allow any chemicals applied to the body, such as lotions and deodorants, to dry on your skin to minimize their impact on the fabric. This is especially important for creams or oil-based products.

The key to stain removal is immediate attention; the longer a stain is allowed to set the more difficult it is to remove. Consult a dry cleaner for treating fine or delicate fabrics.

Dry Cleaning: Take your cue from men and only dry-clean suits, jackets, and similar items not worn close to the skin four to six times a year. Frequent dry cleaning can lead to fabric damage and a shorter useful life.

- Always clean all pieces of an outfit together to prevent premature discoloration or fading of one piece over another. Also, if the item is stained, be sure to point out the stain to the cleaners and tell them what it is to avoid unnecessary chemical treatment

- Don't forget to point out special details on garments to minimize the risk of finding them damaged or missing. The cleaners can put coverings on ornate buttons or other details to protect them during the dry cleaning process

- Bulk cleaning works for sweaters and other items that do not require pressing

- Waterproofing needs to be done at least once a year in order to preserve water repellency

Cleaning at Home: Never underestimate the need to follow care label instructions. You may feel that you know what is best; but today many garments are fashioned from fabrics with many fiber combinations, making the choice of cleaning (for instance, machine versus hand washing) very important.

Many manufacturers suggest turning machine washable items inside-out to reduce stress on the garment. It may be a good practice to do this with all items.

The zippered mesh bags found in the notions department of drugstores are great for hosiery, delicate blouses, or lingerie. Bras should always be clasped shut to prevent them from snagging on other garments in the wash.

Shoes, boots, and handbags: Before wearing shoes or boots for the first time, apply paste polish to form a protective barrier that will increase the life of the leather. Suede needs the application of a stain-repellent spray. These tips apply to handbags as well. If shoes get wet, stuff them with crumpled newspaper and allow them to dry completely away from direct heat. Afterwards they can be polished to look like new.

Just as clothes need rest, so, too, do shoes. If at all possible, let a day pass between wearings. When shoes show signs of age, revitalize them by replacing soles, heels, or possibly having them dyed a darker shade.

Conclusion

Mastering Your Professional Image was written to provide you with the framework you need to enhance your physical image. It embraces one absolute fact, that whatever effort is put forth or choices are made in regard to your personal appearance you must allow your personality to come forth.

You are an individual, with a unique personality. But you are also a physical being. And, if you choose to take your abilities and knowledge out into the working world, you will need a definite plan of action to help ensure you get what you want.

All the elements necessary for an effective action plan are at your fingertips in *Mastering Your Professional Image*. Throughout the book you are given fundamental concepts and definitions by which you may understand what 'professional image' is and what the various elements of style include. From this, you will be able to design a wardrobe that not only reflects your personality and style, but is also appropriate for most business situations and will give you the most value for your clothing budget.

In the first section, Defining Your Options provided details regarding four Classic, timeless styles of dressing. You are given information on the benefits of each style and how the style can impact a situation. Slight differences in color, fabric, or shape will take you from one style to another. You can maximize your visual presentation by knowing how, when, and why to choose a certain style of dressing. Each of the Classics may reflect new fashion trends, but will never change as categorical styles of dressing. To know and understand these basic styles is fundamental information for every woman to use throughout her lifetime.

Enhancing Your Image first tells you how to interpret and understand your body's proportions and how the fit of the clothes may enhance certain body types and dimensions. You should be better able to understand exactly what type of clothing, fabric, and color maximizes your unique figure. By using this information, you can select clothes that evoke a significantly attractive physical appearance, one that capitalizes on your natural physical attributes and minimizes those aspects of your body type that need not draw attention. Next, you discovered the importance of accessories and how they can be used to define your personality, allow you to express creativity, and provide essential detail to your wardrobe. Finally, elements of good grooming are defined and suggestions offered to ensure even the smallest grooming details are part of your daily practice. Attention to these details resounds in the professional situation, where physical grooming is often viewed as a clue to how one will approach and carry out the task at hand.

In Mastering Special Situations, you are shown how to adapt your look to fit the unique character of various parts of the United States as well as other parts of the world. Also, you are given valuable information and suggestions regarding dress selection and particularities of out-of-office locations, such as public speaking engagements and presentations, television appearances, and the anxiety-laden job interview. Adjusting your dress style, for example, color and fabric choice, to accommodate the camera allows you to present yourself in the best way possible. You can dress to be heard and remembered.

In the last three sections, Achieving an Effective Wardrobe, No-Nonsense Shopping, and Doubling Your Investment, you are given a comprehensive outline of activities and procedures to identify, examine, and maintain a personal wardrobe. Thorough analysis and organization of your closets are described, with the intention of arriving at a wardrobe depicting a personal dress style rather than a closet of outdated, mismatched, or impulse-purchased clothing. Once your 'basic' wardrobe is defined, shopping strategies are given to help you build your wardrobe in an organized manner with an awareness of purchasing for the requirements of completing a wardrobe, not merely purchasing for the sake of purchasing. Finally, information is provided that allows a lasting return on the investment you have made. By changing the ways in which you store and maintain your clothes, you can add years of wear and vitality to most items.

We hope you have enjoyed reading *Mastering Your Professional Image.* Consistent application of these ideas and concepts will give you the added confidence of knowing that your image and appearance in the professional world is an accurate reflection of your capabilities and value. Don't be surprised if you find yourself reaching for this book often, especially if you are defining your individuality by making use of more than one style of dressing. Remember, this a resource book for you to use again and again.

Glossary

Balance	Making two things seem equal in size and weight
Batik	Indonesian method of dying fabrics wherein waxed areas resist dye leaving colors in unwaxed areas
Blazer	A semi-fitted single- or double-breasted jacket with two or three outside pockets often with embroidered emblem on left pocket, metal buttons, and hemline ending below the buttocks
Cardigan	Front closing jacket resembling a sweater, usually buttoned and collarless
Challis	Napped fabric of light worsted wool, spun rayon, or blends, usually with printed designs
Clutch Bag	Handbag designed to be tucked under the arm, often featuring a detachable strap or handle
Dirndl	A slim skirt with gathers into the waistband
Envelope	Handbag designed with an accordion- or French-crease bottom
Empire	Dress with a high waistline just under the bust, defined by an inserted piece of fabric or seam
Flannel	A loosely woven fabric with napped surface, primarily wool or cotton
Fleur-de-lis	French stylized lily design used in heraldry and part of the coat-of-arms of the French royal family
Gabardine	A durable, closely woven fabric with definite diagonal ridges; fabric can be wool, cotton, rayon, or synthetic
Hidden Support	In jackets or coats a shape that is permanently established by using a firm interfacing and shoulder emphasis
Jacquard	A process that produces an all-over or sectional design of color or texture in fabric
Jewel Neck	A plain round neckline at the base of the throat used in sweaters, blouses, dresses, and some jackets
Kick Pleats	Single flat pleat or an inverted pleat at the center back of the skirt to make walking easier
Khaki Color	Yellowish-olive-brown
Madras	A hand-loomed Indian cotton with plaids, checks, and stripes all colorfully intermingled
Notched Lapel	A fairly wide V-shaped opening at the outside edge of the seam between the collar and the lapel

Paisley	A fabric pattern of colorful curvy shapes (stylized flowers, pears, leaves, etc.)
Patina	The sheen produced by age
Peaked Lapel	Jacket or coat lapel that comes to a point at the outer edges
Peplum	A short flounce attached to the close-fitting waistband of a jacket or blouse
Pima Cotton	Fine quality cotton raised in the southern U.S. or Mexico
Polo	A knitted pullover shirt with attached collar and front button placket
Proportion	A ratio when one thing is compared to another
Satchel	Leather bag on a rigid flat bottom, with sides sloped to close on metal frame; similar to bags carried by doctors
Serge	A sturdy woolen woven fabric with a diagonal rib on both sides used for suits, coats, jackets, and skirts
Scale	A defined ratio for comparing sizes, or keeping sizes in relationship to one another
Silk Crepe de chine	Fine lightweight silk with crepe texture
Set-in sleeve	Tailored sleeves set smoothly into the armhole
Shirtwaist	Men's shirt style combined with a skirt
Single-breasted	A jacket variation of the blazer without outside pockets or metal buttons
Spectator Shoes	A pump, sling, or lace-up flat in two-toned leather, usually black, brown, or navy on white. The darker trim covers the toe and sometimes the heel
Tapestry	Woven designs in vari-colored scenes
Tartan	A woolen fabric with a plaid pattern distinctive to a Scottish highland clan
Tunic	A long top reaching below the hips to mid-thigh
Twill	A type of weave with a diagonal rib so fine that it may be difficult to see; durable fabrics of wool, rayon, and cotton
Vamp	The upper part of a shoe or boot covering the instep and sometimes extending over the toe
Wool Crepe	Lightweight fabric with a slight pebbly texture

Bibliography

Ailes, Roger with Kraisher, Jon. *You Are The Message, Getting What You Want By Being Who You Are*. New York: Doubleday, 1988.

The American Heritage Dictionary. 2nd ed. Boston: Houghton Mifflin Co., 1985.

Bixler, Susan, *The Professional Image*. New York: G.P. Putnam's Sons, 1984.

Bixler, Susan. *Professional Presence*. New York: G.P. Putnam's Sons, 1991.

Brown, Lillian. *Your Public Best: The Complete Guide to Making Successful Public Appearances*. New York: Newmarket Press, 1989.

Calasibetta, Charlotte, Dr., Ph.D. *Fairchild's Dictionary of Fashion*. New York: Fairchild Publications, Inc., 1975.

Evatt, Crislynne. *How to Organize Your Closet...And Your Life!* San Francisco: Etheos, 1980.

Florin, Gail. *Your Ideal Silhouette, Body Proportion Analysis*. Bloomington, Illinois: Meridian Education Corporation, 1991.

Fujii, Donna with von Alten, Judith Walthers. *Color With Style*. Tokyo: Graphic-Sha Publishing Company, Ltd., 1991.

Gray, James Jr. *The Winning Image*. New York: AMACOM, American Management Association, 1993.

Houck, Catherine. *The Fashion Encyclopedia*. New York: St. Martin's Press, 1982.

Johnson, Jeane G., and Foster, Anne G. *Clothing Image And Impact*, 2nd ed. Cincinnati, Ohio: South-Western Publishing Company, 1990.

Keltner, Vicki, and Holsey, Mike. *The Success Image*. Houston: Gulf Publishing Company, 1982.

Larkey, Jan. *Flatter Your Figure*. New York: Prentice Hall Press, 1991.

Leopold, Allison Kyle, and Cloutier, Anne Marie. *Short Chic*. New York: A Bantam Book/ published by arrangement with Rawson, Wade Publishers, Inc., 1983.

Lucas, Jacqui, and Lundell, Coralyn. *You and Your Image*. Los Gatos, California: Twoells Publishing, 1991.

Mathis, Carla Mason, and Connor, Helen Villa. *The Triumph of Individual Style*. Cali, Columbia: Timeless Additions, 1993.

Michelle, Colette. *Look Like a Million*. San Diego: Fashion Promotions Unlimited, 1981, 1982, 1986.

Parsons, Alyce, and Parente, Diane. *Universal Style*. Ross, California: Parente & Parsons, 1991.

Patton, E. Jean, with Brett, Jacqueline Cantey. *Color to Color: The Black Woman's Guide to a Rainbow of Fashion and Beauty*. New York: A Fireside Book published by Simon & Schuster, 1991.

Pickney, Gerrie, and Swenson, Marge. *Your New Image, Through Color and Line*. Costa Mesa, California: Fashion Image/Crown Summit Books, 1981.

Rasband, Judith. *Fabulous Fit*. New York: Fairchild Publications, 1994.

Rasband, Judith. *Your Business Photo, Pitfalls to Avoid, Pointers to Observe*. Provo, Utah: Personal/Professional Image Consultants, a division of Home Management House, 1987.

Reid, T.J. *Accessory Advantage Handbook*. Amite, Louisiana: T.J.'s For Her, Inc., 1993.

Straley, Carol. *Sensational Scarves*. New York: Prince Paperbacks, Crown Publishers, Inc., 1985.

Thompson, Jacqueline, Ed. *Image Impact*. New York: A&W Publishers, Inc., 1981.

Wallace, Joanne. *Dress with Style*. Old Tappan, New Jersey: Fleming H. Revell Company, 1983.

Weiland, Barbara, and Wood, Leslie. *Clothes Sense*. Portland, Oregon: Palmer/Pletsch Associates, 1984.

Index

J

J. Crew, 33

J.G. Hook, 9

J.H. Collectibles, 9

Jackets
arrangement in closet, 112
asymmetrical, 22
blazer, 6, 30, 51
bomber, 30, 55
cardigan, 30, 51
collar-less, 6, 14, 20
cropped, 20, 38, 55
double-breasted, 6, 14, 20
fit. See Fit
length. See Length
peplum, 38
single-breasted, 6, 14, 22, 30
for specific Classic styles, 6, 14, 20, 30
for specific Non-Classic styles, 38, 42
tunic, 14, 20

Jaeger, 17

Japan, international dressing, 100

Jewel colors
message behind wearing, 75
for specific cities, 97, 99

Jewelry
for petites, 71
for plus-sizes, 73
shopping for, 81-90
for specific Classic styles, 10, 18, 26, 34
for specific Non-Classic styles, 38, 42, 46
storage of, 126
and travel, 101

Job interview, 107

Jones of New York, 9

K

Kinsel, Brenda, 80

Knits, storage of, 125

L

Latin America, international dressing, 100

Laura Ashley, 38

Legs
hemline, effect on, 61
hosiery, for emphasis or to de-emphasize, 61, 82
shoes to complement, 82
special considerations for public speaking, 106

Length
jackets, appropriate for, 61
pants, appropriate for, 62
shoes, coordinating with, 82
skirts, appropriate for, 61
for specific cities, 98-99

Lipstick, 92

Liz Clairborne, 33

Lizsport, 33

Los Angeles, regional dressing, 99

M

Maggiore, Evana, 97

Makeup, 91-92. See also Grooming
for special situations, 104-107

Measurements. See Fit

Message
of being conservative and a team player, 3-5
of being distinctive and stand-out, 3, 20-21
of being genteel and supportive, 37
of being glamorous and suggestive, 41
of being imaginative and spontaneous, 45
of being refined and in subtle but firm control, 3, 12-13
of being relaxed and approachable, 3, 28-29
of colors, 75-77

Michaels, Angie, 97

Middle East, international dressing, 100

Monochromatic, 15, 78

Moth proofing, 126

N

Nails and hands, 93

Nanfeldt, Suzan, 72-73

Natural fibers, 79

Necklaces
for balancing the length of the neck, 88
lengths, 88
for specific Classic styles, 10, 18, 35
for specific Non-Classic styles, 38

Necklines
for specific Classic styles, 6, 14, 20, 30
for specific Non-Classic styles, 38, 42

Neutral colors
message behind wearing, 75
shoes, 113
for specific cities, 97, 99

New York, regional dressing, 97

Non-Classic styles. See , Alluring; Creative; Feminine

O

Orange, 77

Mastering Your Professional Image™
DRESSING TO ENHANCE YOUR CREDIBILITY
by Diane Parente and Stephanie Petersen

Women are no longer limited to one professional look!
Mastering Your Professional Image will guide you to finding the best look
for your visual presentation in a variety of business situations.

It is a resource guide and advice book all in one.

- -

Please send me _____ copy(s) of *Mastering Your Professional Image* by Parente and Petersen for $19.95 plus $5.00 to cover sales tax, shipping and handling. Enclosed is my check or money order for $_____ made payable to Image Development and Management, Inc.

Name _____

Address _____

_____

Phone _____

How did you hear about the book? _____

_____

Mail To: Image Development and Management, Inc.
Post Office Box 262
Ross, CA 94957

(415) 258-0285   fax (415) 485-1793

The Authors

Diane Parente is president of Image Development and Management, Inc., a diversified, innovative firm providing result-oriented image programs for businesses. With more than twenty years of experience as a recognized expert, she continuously consults with professionals in finance, marketing, media, law, medicine, hospitality, and direct sales.

Diane has twice received the highest awards of excellence from the two major industry groups, the Association of Image Consultants International (AICI) and Image Industry Council International.

Over the past five years Diane has co-authored two books on image, serves on the Foothill College Advisory Committee, is a member of the National Speakers Association, and the Association of Image Consultants International.

Stephanie Petersen, M.B.A., J.D., and member of the California Bar Association, is the director of municipal investment research at a major national discount brokerage company. Over the last fifteen years she has successfully used the methods in *Mastering Your Professional Image* to enhance her career and add to her overall effectiveness.

Illustrator

Jan Mucklestone, of Los Altos, CA., is an accomplished illustrator who has worked with many notable personalities, including Edith Head at Universal Studios. Jan founded Illustration Design in 1980, and devotes her time to creating illustrations for manufacturers, specialty retailers and private commissions. In early 1996, Jan expects to release her two recently completed CD-ROM illustration products.